EDGAR ALLAN POE

Other titles in the **Americans: The Spirit of a Nation** *series:*

ABRAHAM LINCOLN

"This Nation Shall Have a New Birth of Freedom"

ISBN-13: 978-0-7660-3170-8
ISBN-10:   0-7660-3170-5

CLARA BARTON

"Face Danger, But Never Fear It"

ISBN-13: 978-0-7660-3024-4
ISBN-10:   0-7660-3024-5

MATHEW BRADY

"The Camera Is the Eye of History"

ISBN-13: 978-0-7660-3023-7
ISBN-10:   0-7660-3023-7

P. T. BARNUM

"Every Crowd Has a Silver Lining"

ISBN-13: 978-0-7660-3022-0
ISBN-10:   0-7660-3022-9

AMERICANS
THE *Spirit* OF A *Nation*

EDGAR ALLAN POE

"Deep Into That Darkness Peering"

Jeff Burlingame

Enslow Publishers, Inc.
40 Industrial Road
Box 398
Berkeley Heights, NJ 07922
USA

http://www.enslow.com

To my wife, Lisa: I see no Heaven—but in your eyes.

Copyright © 2009 by Jeff Burlingame

Library of Congress Cataloging-in-Publication Data:

Burlingame, Jeff.
    Edgar Allan Poe : "deep into that darkness peering" / Jeff Burlingame.
        p. cm. — (Americans—the spirit of a nation)
        Includes bibliographical references and index.
        Summary: "Examines the emotionally turbulent life of author and poet Edgar Allan Poe, including his brilliant stories and poems and his many contributions to the literary world"—Provided by publisher.
    ISBN-13: 978-0-7660-3020-6
    ISBN-10: 0-7660-3020-2
        1. Poe, Edgar Allan, 1809–1849—Juvenile literature. 2. Authors, American—19th century—Biography—Juvenile literature. I. Title.
    PS2631.B87 2008
    818'.309—dc22
    [B]
                                      2007041343

Printed in the United States of America

10 9 8 7 6 5 4 3 2 1

Illustration Credits: Courtesy and copyright Bob Travis, pp. 13, 17; Courtesy Jim Veneman, p. 53; Courtesy of Josh Berglund, Flickr.com, p. 36; Enoch Pratt Free Library, pp. 3, 51; Enslow Publishers, Inc., p. 14; The Everett Collection, p. 101; The Granger Collection, New York, p. 42; From *Israfel: The Life and Times of Edgar Allan Poe*, published in 1934, pp. 8, 12, 19, 20, 25, 26, 28, 45, 50, 55, 81, 84, 88; iStockphoto.com, p. 91; © 2007 JupiterImages, pp. 64, 107; Library of Congress, pp. 6, 16, 59, 70, 73; Mary Evans Picture Library/ARTHUR RACKHAM/Everett Collection, pp. 11, 24, 46, 57; Mary Evans Picture Library/Everett Collection, pp. 30, 32; Courtesy of The Maryland Historical Society, pp. 94, 104; Nicolle diMella, pp. 96, 103; Public-domain image from Wikipedia.org, p. 75; Shutterstock.com, pp. 22, 108; Valentine Richmond History Center, p. 34.

Cover Illustration: Library of Congress.

CONTENTS

Edgar Allan Poe

1

A Grand Prize

Edgar Allan Poe was desperate. Cast from the home of his wealthy foster father, the struggling writer was living with the only people who would have him—poor relatives who themselves were barely making ends meet. Adding another mouth to feed nearly crippled the cramped household, especially the mouth of a young man capable of working and helping out. Poe understood this and was feeling the guilt of being a burden.

Guilt, then worry, finally spurred Poe to action. He began writing letters to anyone he thought could help him get a job. He wrote to one newspaper owner: "I write to request your influence in obtaining some situation or employment in this city . . . Salary would be a minor consideration, but I do not wish to be idle."[1] The owner did not respond. Several more attempts to make a living as a writer also failed. Nervous and humbled, Poe swallowed his pride.

As he often did when he felt he had no other options, Poe turned to his foster father, John Allan, for help. From an attic room with a ceiling so low it was impossible to stand up straight, Poe wrote another letter. In near-perfect cursive, he wrote he was "without friends."[2] He wrote that he could not find a job and was "perishing" because no one would help him.[3] He ended the letter with, "For God's sake pity me, and save me from destruction."[4]

Poe often turned to his foster father, John Allan (above), for help, especially when he needed money.

In John Allan's mind, any "destruction" that may happen to Poe would be his own fault. The wealthy man had helped Poe most of his life. He took his foster son into his tidy home when Poe was a poor, young orphan. He sent him to the finest schools and gave him money when he needed it as an adult. He had bailed him out of many difficult situations. But he felt Poe was unappreciative and did not make good decisions or learn from his mistakes. So Allan eventually quit helping. As far as he was concerned, Poe had messed up too many opportunities. He thought his foster son was a failure. As sad as Poe's words sounded, Allan did not reply to the letter.

But Allan did jot his thoughts on the back of a previous letter from Poe. He said his foster son had the "deepest ingratitude," an uncaring heart, and no honor.[5] He said Poe's main skill, writing, would never pay the bills. He would rather Poe become a business-man like he was. In his mind, that was the safest path to happiness and success. But Poe had little interest in playing it safe, and the foster father lost faith in his son.

The two had not spoken for three years before Poe sent his desperate letter. He mostly wrote when he wanted something. It had worked several times, but it appeared he would never again receive charity from Allan. Now twenty-four years old, Poe had to make a tough choice if he wanted to survive. He could follow his foster father's advice and become a businessman, laborer, or a skilled tradesman. Or he could continue to try and make it as a writer, doing what most thought he could not. Poe had been trying to do that for several years. He had published three books of poetry. But they made him little money. Attempts to get paying jobs failed. Still, he kept trying.

Shortly after sending the letter begging his foster father for help, Poe entered six stories in a writing contest. His thrilling tale of a stormy shipwreck, "MS. Found in a Bottle," won first place in the fiction contest. The prize was fifty dollars, a rather large sum of money in 1833. Today, that would equal about twelve hundred dollars. It certainly was enough money to make a large contribution to his poor household.

Even more important than the money was the boost to Poe's self-esteem and the new opportunities he received. It earned Poe some important supporters. One of the contest's judges, John Pendleton Kennedy, helped Poe land a steady job as a magazine editor. Another judge, John Latrobe, was impressed with Poe when they met. Latrobe later described their first meeting, saying, "On most men his clothes would have looked shabby and seedy, but there was something about this man that prevented one from criticising his garments."[6] His clothes may have been in bad shape, but Poe's enthusiasm and talent for writing helped him make a good impression. Despite continuous setbacks, Poe never lost confidence in his writing ability.

Shortly after Poe's big triumph in the contest, his foster father died. Poe always assumed that if he did not succeed at writing, John Allan's death would make him wealthy. He thought Allan would leave him a large sum

An illustrated version of "MS. Found in a Bottle" was published in Tales of Mystery *in 1935. This depiction of two extremely elderly seamen was done by Arthur Rackham.*

Poe's prize-winning story, "MS. Found in a Bottle," first appeared in the October 19, 1833 edition of the Saturday Visiter *newspaper.*

of money when he died. Instead, Poe got nothing. Allan had not forgiven Poe and left him out of his will. Now, more than ever, Poe would have to take care of himself. If he wanted to become one of the greatest writers in history, as he always said he did, it was not going to be easy. In Poe's life, nothing ever was.

Chapter
2

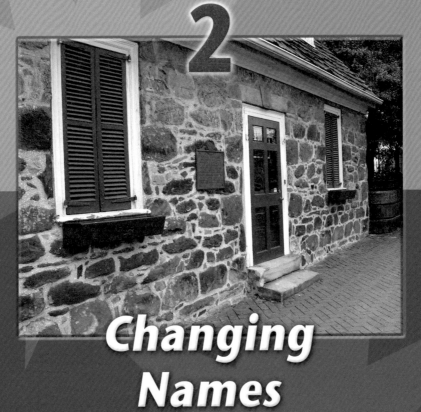

Changing
Names

Being an actor or actress two hundred years ago was nothing like it is today. There was none of Hollywood's glitz or glamour. There were no bright lights or big-screen TVs, no million-dollar movie contracts. In the early 1800s, there mostly were simple stages to act on. Little pay was available. To earn it, actors had to travel from city to city to perform on different stages each night.

Because the lifestyle was difficult, people who acted did so mainly because they loved entertaining others. That is exactly what Eliza Poe was doing

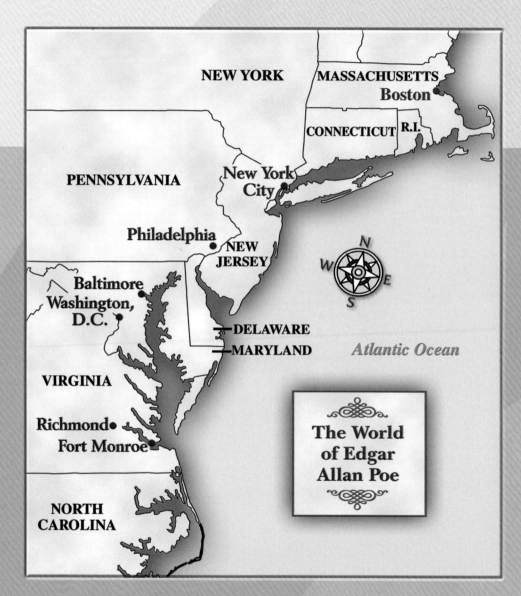

NEW YORK

MASSACHUSETTS
Boston

CONNECTICUT R.I.

PENNSYLVANIA

New York
City

Philadelphia

NEW
JERSEY

Baltimore
Washington,
D.C.

DELAWARE

MARYLAND

Atlantic Ocean

VIRGINIA

Richmond
Fort Monroe

N
W E
S

The World
of Edgar
Allan Poe

NORTH
CAROLINA

This map of the eastern region of the United States shows many of the places that Poe lived in and traveled to during his life.

when her second son, Edgar, was born in Boston on January 19, 1809. At the time, she and her husband, David Poe, Jr., were part of a troupe of actors. They performed up and down the east coast of the United States. They acted in the big cities of Boston, New York, and Philadelphia. They also performed in many smaller towns.

Two Actors

Eliza Poe had been acting since she was a young child. She and her mother had even moved to the United States from England to continue their acting careers. Now, Eliza Poe was one of the most successful actresses on the circuit. Newspaper reviews of her performances were almost always positive. Critics loved her talent and good looks. They loved her beautiful dancing and singing. One wrote she had a "sweetly melodious voice when she charms us with a song."[1] Another wrote, ". . . the lady was young and pretty."[2] She was the star in many plays and, occasionally, performed her own concerts.[3]

David Poe's acting was not as good as his wife's. He did receive some positive reviews. But newspaper critiques of his work were often negative. One even called him "wretched."[4] The handsome man had once trained to be a lawyer. Many felt he would have been better off if he had stuck with that career choice. Despite this, David Poe managed to find steady work as an actor. Oftentimes, he performed alongside his more talented wife, Eliza.

Critics and fans may have been friendly to Eliza Poe, but life outside the theater rarely was. By the time Edgar was born when she was twenty-two, she had already suffered tremendously. She had no memories of her father, who died when she was two. She had few memories of her mother, who died when she was eleven. She was raised by the troupe of actors she traveled with. Eliza married at age fifteen, but three years later, her husband died. Shortly after, she married Edgar's father, David Poe. He had seen her on stage and, like many others, had fallen for her incredible charm.

Eliza Poe was a successful actress. In her day, actors had to travel to perform in different shows throughout the country.

Abandoned

After she met her second husband, Eliza Poe's misfortune appeared to be a thing of the past. The couple settled in Boston and found steady acting jobs at a theater there. They had two children, William Henry and Edgar. Life seemed as if it were going to work out well.

However, when Edgar still was very young, David Poe abandoned him, his brother, and his mother. No one is certain why. Most believe he was not happy with his life for some reason. His family never heard from

The Poe Museum in Richmond, Virginia, is located in The Old Stone House, which is only a few blocks away from Poe's first home.

him again. Some historians think he died soon after he fled. Others say he started a new life elsewhere with a different family. It is possible he finally became the lawyer he originally had intended to be.

Eliza Poe continued acting. She gave birth to her third child, Rosalie, in December 1810. It is uncertain whether David Poe was Rosalie's father or if someone else was. By that time, Eliza Poe and her three children were living in Richmond, Virginia. The fatherless family struggled, living off the mother's acting wages and charity given to them by friends and fans. Many people in the community felt sorry for them.

Loss of a Mother

An impoverished life was not all Eliza Poe had to deal with. Soon, she became ill. It was noticeable onstage. For the first time in her life, the beautiful and talented actress began receiving poor reviews. She eventually became too sick to act. She had to rely solely on charity to survive and support her three children.

On November 29, 1811, an article in the city's newspaper read, "On this night, *Mrs. Poe*, lingering on the bed of disease and surrounded by her children, asks your assistance and *asks it for perhaps the last time*."[5] It turns out the paper was correct. Less than two weeks later, on December 8, with her three young children at her bedside, Eliza Poe died. She was only twenty-four years old. Each of her children's lives, including

Eliza Poe's "Consumption"

The common belief is that Edgar Allan Poe's mother died of "consumption," now known as tuberculosis. Symptoms can include a cough, sometimes with blood; a swollen neck; rapid heartbeat; fever; muscle weakness; and shortness of breath.[6]

Today, this bacterial disease of the lungs is treated with antibiotics. But modern antibiotics, like penicillin, had not been discovered at the time of Eliza Poe's death.

two-year-old Edgar's, were now going to be lived like much of hers was—as an orphan.

The mother left her three young children no money and very few material items. Edgar received a painting of Boston Harbor. On the back it said, "For my little son Edgar, who should ever love Boston, the place of his birth, and where his mother found her best, and most *sympathetic* friends."[7]

Frances Allan (above) and John Allan married in 1803.

New Parents

Without a mother or father to care for them, the Poe children needed a place to live and people to raise them. William Henry, almost five years old, was sent to Baltimore, Maryland. Relatives of his missing father cared for him there. One-year-old Rosalie went to live with a local family named Mackenzie.

Nearly three, Edgar went to live with John and Frances "Fanny" Allan. The Allans had been fans of the young child's mother. John Allan had one child born to another woman before he married, but he and Fanny Allan had no children together. They never officially adopted Edgar. But they still added their last name to his.

The boy's new name was Edgar Allan Poe.

Early Talent

Moving in with the Allans was a big change for Edgar. He and his family had been living in poverty and were used to taking handouts. The Allans were doing fine financially. John Allan was a successful Richmond businessman. He made his money, in large part, by selling tobacco and shipping it to Europe. Then he would buy European goods and sell them in America. Like Edgar, John Allan had been an orphan. But he overcame that obstacle and made a good life for himself and his family.

A New Life

Fanny Allan had a lot in common with Edgar's mother, and even looked like her. She also had been an orphan. Naturally, she and her husband had soft spots for Edgar's sad situation. They could relate to what he was going through. So, as focused as John Allan was on his business, his wife's pressure made him agree to take Edgar into their home.

Once they decided to care for him, the Allans were quick to treat Edgar as their own. They dressed him nicely in suits costing five dollars each.[1] Today, that would be the same as a child wearing an eighty-dollar outfit, not including shoes. Edgar was sent to the finest schools. The new family vacationed together. Though he was without a mother and separated from his brother and sister, Edgar's life was better in many ways. He now had a family with a stable income. He was never hungry. He was no longer in a family that had to rely on charity from strangers.

When Edgar was six, he and the Allans traveled across the Atlantic Ocean by boat to Britain. John Allan had been born in Scotland and was going to England to start a branch of his business.

Living in England

While living in Britain, Edgar attended boarding schools, or schools where students live as well as study. They were more expensive than regular schools, but provided a better education than other schools of the

Tobacco Farming

Though he likely never gave it much thought, John Allan owed the American Indians thanks for part of his successful business, which included tobacco along with other products. When Europeans traveled across the Atlantic Ocean and began exploring America in the early 1600s, they discovered American Indians smoking tobacco, which did not exist in Europe. Leaves of the plant were soon taken to Europe,

Tobacco leaves hang to dry.

where it became popular to smoke tobacco. It was said to have miraculous healing powers when used in large amounts.[2]

By 1691, tobacco was the leading export of the colony of Virginia. Many businessmen moved there to try and make money from growing, harvesting, and selling the crop.[3] Plantation owners bought slaves to do most of the labor. Of course, tobacco smoking is now banned in many public places across the United States due to its harmful effects. But in Edgar Allan Poe's time, those effects were unknown. Many people smoked tobacco. Those who sold it, as Poe's foster father did, often made a lot of money.

time. The Misses Dubourg, the daughters of Francis Dubourg, ran Edgar's first boarding school. Edgar later used the name Dubourg for a character in one of his most famous stories, "The Murders in the Rue Morgue." Not much is known about his time spent in school with the Misses Dubourg. But Edgar was said to be "quite well" during that time.[4]

The Reverend John Bransby ran the next school Edgar attended. Edgar later wrote about that experience in a story called "William Wilson." The Reverend Bransby did not like the story. It described the schoolhouse as creepy. It said the rules were too strict. Bransby felt it made the school look far worse than it actually was. His teacher later called Edgar, ". . . a quick and clever boy and would have been a very good boy if he had not been spoilt by his parents."[5]

Edgar lived a few years in London, England, while Allan's business was successful. But many businesses began to fail in 1819. Allan's did, too. He found himself heavily in debt. He decided to abandon his attempt to make a business work in his homeland. When Edgar was eleven, he and his family sailed for more than a month back across the ocean to Richmond, Virginia. It was 1820, and it took them thirty-one days to get back to the United States. Fanny Allan, for one, was happy to return. While in England, she often was ill.[6]

Back Home

Edgar returned to Richmond better educated than most of his peers. He could speak French. According to

Edgar Allan Poe used the last name of the sisters who ran his first boarding school in his story "The Murders in the Rue Morgue." Above is an illustration from an edition of the story published in 1935.

historian Jeffrey Myers, he also was "far better acquainted with history and literature than many boys of a more advanced age."[7] Because of the family's recent financial problems, Edgar did not attend a boarding school when he returned. Instead, he lived at home and went to an all-boys school each morning. His peers considered him athletic: good at running, jumping, and swimming. As gifted as he was at those activities, Edgar was even better at writing poetry. Before he was twelve, his foster father showed his teacher some of Edgar's poems that the boy wanted to publish into a book.[8] The teacher did not allow that to happen. He felt Edgar was

Edgar Allan Poe attended the Manor House School at Stoke Newington in London, England, from 1817 to 1820.

Flow softly—gently—vital
stream;
   Ye crimson life drops, stay;
Indulge me with this pleasing
dream
   Thro' an eternal day

See—see—my soul, hence going!
see how her eye balls glare!
Those shrieks delightful harmony
Proclaim her deep despair.

Rise—rise e'infernal spirits, rise,
swift dart across her brain
O thau Horror with blood chilling cries
loud on thy hideous train

O, feast my soul revenge is sweet
   Louisa, take my scorn;—
Curs'd was the hour that saw us
        meet
The hour when we were born

4 Sp

Many historians think this poem was written by Edgar Allan Poe when he was a youth. The poem was found in the early twentieth century by Professor Killis Campbell.

already too vain.[9] Publishing a book, the teacher believed, would only make Edgar think he was even more superior than he already did.

The family's financial situation did not improve back in the United States. They had to move in with John Allan's business partner for a while before getting a small cottage nearby. Allan's debts made it so life was not as luxurious as it had been before the family left the country. He was still repaying what he had borrowed in England.

Another Loss

Fanny Allan's health did not improve much upon returning home, either. Being sick made it difficult for her to be a good mother. It was hard for her to pay attention to an excitable teenage boy who wanted to explore and learn about the world. Edgar soon turned to Jane Stanard for motherly advice and affection. She was the mother of a friend.

Like his schoolteachers in England, Stanard also later became a subject of Edgar's writings. As an adult, he wrote the love poem "To Helen" about her. Helen obviously was not her name but she inspired the poem. Some believe Poe picked the title because of Helen of Troy, a character in Greek mythology and the daughter of gods. Helen of Troy was said to be so beautiful that a major war was started over her. That was the way Poe felt about Stanard. In "To Helen," he compares Stanard's beauty to a boat sailing gently over a "perfumed sea."[10]

However, Stanard died at a young age. At fifteen, Edgar lost another important woman in his life.

First Love

It did not take Edgar long after Jane Stanard's death to find another female to focus on. In 1825, now sixteen, he fell in love with his neighbor's daughter. The fifteen-year-old girl's name was Elmira Royster. Elmira later said of Edgar, "He was a beautiful boy . . . he was warm and zealous in any cause he was interested in."[11] She also said Edgar could sing well, just like his birth

Elmira Royster was the first girl that Edgar Allan Poe loved.

mother, who had been praised by all who heard her. Edgar and Elmira became secretly engaged. Until the girl's father found out, that is. He did not approve because Elmira and Edgar were too young, and broke off the relationship. Edgar later wrote the poem "Song" about Elmira. In it, he talks about how beautiful he imagines her to be on her "bridal day" he did not get to see.[12]

Elmira was not the only one to find young Edgar "beautiful." Many girls did. Throughout his life, especially when he was a young adult, women were attracted to the slender man. Standing about five feet, eight inches tall, Edgar's posture was nearly perfect. His eyes, depending on whose report you believe, were either gray, violet, or hazel. The few black-and-white photographs taken of Poe show a man with dark, possibly black, hair and dark eyes. There were also two watercolor paintings and an oil painting done of Poe in his lifetime. One watercolorist gave him gray eyes. The oil painter gave him hazel eyes. His hair was brown in all the paintings.

Elmira later wrote more about her experience with Edgar Allan Poe. She said he was:

> . . . *not very talkative. When he did talk though he was pleasant but his general manner was sad. . . . [He] was very generous. . . . He had strong prejudices. Hated anything coarse and unrefined. Never spoke of his [real] parents. . . . [He was] very enthusiastic and impulsive.*[13]

Edgar was not in Richmond when Elmira's father broke off the young couple's engagement. By then, he was nearly seventy miles away. He was on his own for the first time, discovering what the world had to offer an athletic, educated, and impulsive boy with an enormous talent for writing.

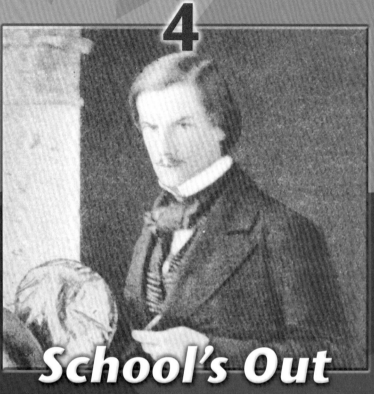

Chapter 4

School's Out

The University of Virginia has housed its share of famous people. Well-known politicians, such as President Woodrow Wilson, have gone to school there. Many popular athletes, astronauts, and entertainers have, too. The school has a rich tradition. But, in 1826, that was not yet true. Located in the small city of Charlottesville, the university was then only one year old. Less than two hundred students went to school there. That February, seventeen-year-old Edgar Allan Poe became one of them.

A Young College

Thomas Jefferson, who had written the Declaration of Independence, and later became the third president of the United States, created the university several years after his presidency ended. Jefferson had long wanted to build a school where students could get a liberal, or broad, education. Most universities of the time were strict with religion, student behavior, and what students had to study. The University of Virginia offered freedom of choice. It was the perfect place for young adults looking to figure out their lives—away from their parents.

Because it was new, the university struggled in many areas. Giving young people independence meant there was a lot of immature behavior. Students often fought each other. In a letter to John Allan, Poe wrote, "We have had a great many fights up here lately."[1] He described one fight in vivid detail, saying a fighter's arm was "bitten from the shoulder to the elbow."[2] At least once, Poe himself got into a big fight with an acquaintance.

Fighting was not the only problem facing the students. As they still are at many colleges today, gambling and drinking alcohol were common problems at the University of Virginia. Poe, who was younger than most students, quickly fell victim to both vices. He drank and gambled with other students. Trouble was, he did not have a job to pay for those things because he was a student. So he became deeply in debt. Poe later said he only gambled because Allan had not given him enough money to pay his bills and other people would

Poe (right) poses with friends Miles George (left) and Thomas Goode Tucker at the University of Virginia.

not lend him any. So gambling was, Poe said, the only way he could try and make money. He wrote that he "became desperate, and gambled."[3]

Ross Baird, a recent president of the University of Virginia's prestigious Raven Society, said, "We don't admire his gambling addiction."[4] But Baird said Poe's life at the university was not all negative. Poe did well at many activities. He was good at athletics. He also excelled on the debate team and at other academic endeavors. Baird said, "Poe as a student embodied many core values of what University of Virginia students hold dear—fellowship with faculty, as he was close with his tutors; academic excellence, as he scored the highest marks on all of his examinations; and fellowship with other students, as he was well-liked and well-respected."[5]

Problems With Money

By the time Poe enrolled at the university, Allan had returned to wealth. He certainly could have afforded to pay for anything his foster son may have needed. A year before Poe started college, Allan's uncle, William Galt, died. Galt was believed to be the richest man in Virginia. Allan inherited several hundred thousand dollars from him.[6] Today, that would equal millions of dollars. After the few years of struggle when his business was not doing so well, Allan suddenly became far richer than he ever had been. In December 1826, Allan traveled the seventy miles to the school. He paid

University- May 1826

Dear Sir,

    I this morning received the clothes you sent me, voz an uniform coat, six yards of striped cloth for pantaloons & four pair of socks. The coat is a beautiful one & fits me exactly. I thought it best not to write till I received the clothes - or I should have written before this. You have heard no doubt of the disturbances in college. Soon after you left here the grand Jury met and put the Students in a terrible fright. - so much so that the lectures were un attended - and those whose names were upon the Sheriffs' list - travelled off into the woods & mountains - taking their beds & provisions along with them - there were about 50 on the list - so you may suppose the college was very well thinn'd - this was the first day of the fright - the second day, "A proclamation" was issued by the faculty forbidding "any student under pain of a major punishment to leave his dormitory between the hours of 8 & 10 P.M. - (at which time the Sheriff would be about) or in any way to assist the lawful authority of the Sheriff". This order however was very little attended to - as the fear of the Faculty could not counterbalance that of the Grand Jury - most of the "indicted" ran off a second time into the woods and upon an examination the next morning by the Faculty - some were reprimanded - some suspended -

some of Poe's bills and took his foster son home. Poe had been at the University of Virginia less than a year.

"It is a shame that his finances prevented him from staying longer," said Ross Baird, the former president of the Raven Society. "On his last night, Poe spoke earnestly with William Wertenbaker, the university librarian, of his deep regret and declared that he was honor-bound to pay every last cent at his earliest opportunity."[7]

Whether it was to keep that word or some other reason, Poe wanted to return to the university. But he never did. Instead, he was back in Richmond, living in the gigantic house his foster father had bought. The house was called Moldavia. It had a beautiful view of a river and forested hills. The two-story house was made of brick, and had high ceilings and wide porches.[8] Poe now was living in a mansion, but he felt like a failure. To add to his misery, his former fiancée, Elmira Royster, was no longer available. Her father had stopped her from marrying Poe, but, less than a year later, she was about to be married to another man. Poe was not happy to be home.

On the Move Again

Poe was also not pleased with his foster father. Allan was incredibly wealthy, but would not allow Poe to return to school. He was not happy with Poe, either. He had given his foster son a great opportunity to be successful. It was far more of an opportunity than he ever had. It was more than Poe would have had if

A Preserved Room and the Raven Society

Edgar Allan Poe attended the University of Virginia less than a year, but his presence still is felt there. The room he lived in at the school is a memorial to him. It is kept much the same way it was when he was a student. Many of the original furnishings are not there, however, because it is said Poe burned them for firewood.[9] On certain occasions, people are allowed to tour the room.

Much of the credit for maintaining Poe's legacy at the school belongs to the Raven Society. "Being elected to the society is one of the highest honors a student or faculty member can receive," said Ross Baird, a former president of the group.[10] The Raven Society was founded in 1904. The group's goal is to further student, faculty, and alumni interaction. It pays for research, provides scholarships for students, and rewards students and faculty for their good deeds. Instead of saying "hello" or "good-bye," the group says "evermore" in tribute to Poe's most famous poem, "The Raven."

almost anyone else had cared for him after his mother died. It certainly was more of an opportunity than he would have had if his mother had lived. Then, he and his siblings likely would have traveled on the tough acting circuit trying to eke out a living. Poe wanted to return to the University of Virginia, but Allan refused to give him the funds.[11]

Feeling unwelcome and unwanted, Poe stayed in Richmond only a few months. In March 1827, he traveled by boat to Boston, the city of his birth and the place his mother said he should always love. But Poe was not returning under good circumstances. He even had to borrow money to get there. Before he left, he wrote, "I have not one cent in the world to provide any food."[12]

Poe Publishes

Boston was nearly two hundred years old when Poe arrived. He was a poor man in a rich city full of tradition. Boston's harbor allowed for easy transport of goods across the Atlantic Ocean to Europe and beyond. Many successful businessmen lived there for that reason. The city was also known for its strong publishing industry. Many believe that is why Poe wanted to go there—to publish poetry, as he had tried to years ago before being blocked by his schoolteacher. This time, a printer in Boston, Calvin F. S. Thomas, agreed to Poe's wishes. The small book was called *Tamerlane and Other Poems*. Poe did not use his name as the author. Instead the book said it was written "By A Bostonian."

The title poem, "Tamerlane," was named after a military leader from the 1300s named Timur. Timur had been involved in many wars but also supported the creativity of artists. Poe's long poem is about love, death, and the beauty that lies in between. It follows a pattern commonly used in poetry, where the end of every other line rhymes. But, unlike many amateur poets, Poe is willing to break from the pattern when the story calls for it:

> *We grew in age—and love—together—*
> *Roaming the forest, and the wild;*
> *My breast her shield in wintry weather—*
> *And, when the friendly sunshine smiled.*
> *And she would mark the opening skies,*
> *I saw no Heaven—but in her eyes.*[13]

Publishing a book is a big accomplishment, especially for someone so young. But hardly anyone noticed *Tamerlane and Other Poems*. Poe earned no money from the book. He was still scrounging to survive.

In the Army

Poe had enlisted in the United States Army just before his first book was published. It was May 1827, and he was eighteen. He lied and said his age was twenty-two. There was no legitimate reason for him to do so. He could have joined the Army either way. Because of that moment, and because Poe occasionally misstated his age in other places, people have often gotten his age wrong. He also lied and said his name was Edgar

James Fenimore Cooper

While Edgar Allan Poe's first book was going virtually unnoticed, another American author, James Fenimore Cooper, was having a great amount of success. Cooper's most famous tale, *The Last of the Mohicans*, became a best-seller in both the United States and Great Britain. The book, set during the French and Indian War (1754–1763), has sold millions of copies. It is required reading in many English literature classes and has been made into a movie several times.

A. Perry. Some historians feel it was because he wanted to disappear and start a new life separate from the one he had back in Richmond—the one where he was so dependent on John Allan.[14]

After Poe received his military training, the Army sent him to South Carolina, then on to Virginia. The scenery of the place where he lived in South Carolina, Sullivan's Island, was later described in his short story "The Gold-Bug." He described the small island as devoid of large trees, and wrote that there were only a few poorly built buildings:

> *This Island is a very singular one. It consists of little else than the sea sand, and is about three miles long. Its breadth at no point exceeds a quarter of a mile. It is separated from the main*

land by a scarcely perceptible creek, oozing its way through a wilderness of reeds and slime, a favorite resort of the marsh hen. The vegetation, as might be supposed, is scant, or at least dwarfish. No trees of any magnitude are to be seen. Near the western extremity, where Fort Moultrie stands, and where are some miserable frame buildings, tenanted, during summer, by the fugitives from Charleston dust and fever . . .[15]

Many soldiers of the time were not able to read and write. This was a reflection of the general population. However, Poe could do both. That helped him in the Army. He was promoted twice, earning the rank of sergeant major. The Army met most of Poe's needs. He had food, shelter, and an income. It was much more than he had before he joined. But he still was not satisfied. He thought he was wasting time. His dream was to make a living as a writer, and he quickly wanted out of the military. But he had signed up for five years and was required to stay. He began devising a plan.

Poe eventually told his commanding officer about his time at the University of Virginia, and that he had been an orphan. He described his battles with his foster father. But to get out of the Army, Poe needed John Allan's permission. Poe wrote letters home to Richmond asking for it, but never received a response. In early 1829, Poe tried a new approach. He said he wanted to enter West Point, a military academy in New York. The school was difficult to get into and he wanted Allan's help. He thought that plan would gain Allan's support. At the end of the letter, Poe wrote, "Give my love to Ma."[16]

"Ma" was, of course, Fanny Allan. Three weeks after the letter was sent, on February 18, 1829, Poe's foster mother died at age forty-three. Poe was allowed to temporarily leave the Army to travel home to Richmond for her funeral. He did not make it in time, and arrived in town a day late. But Fanny's death opened up a soft spot in John Allan's heart. He bought Poe some clothes, and agreed to help him get out of the Army and into West Point. Poe put in his application to the school and waited.

Good Reviews

In the meantime, he traveled to Baltimore. There, he lived in Beltzhoover's Hotel with a cousin, Edward Mosher. In December 1829, a publisher printed 250 copies of Poe's *Al Aaraaf, Tamerlane and Minor Poems.*

"Tamerlane," of course, had already been printed, but "Al Aaraaf" was new, and likely written when Poe was in the Army. It was about the place between heaven and hell where "men suffer no punishment."[17] Unlike his first book, Poe put his real name on this one. Like his first book, he received no money for his work. As his only pay, Poe was given copies to give to friends and reviewers. Articles written about the book generally were positive.

> It was about the place between heaven and hell where "men suffer no punishment."

Poe was not yet twenty-one years old and had published two books. Six months after the second book was published, Poe entered West Point. True to his history, he did not stay there long.

Cadet Poe

Life at West Point was strict. School started at sunrise, then came breakfast and more classes until 4:00 P.M. Military drills took place until sunset, then dinner and classes until after 9:00 P.M.[18] Bedtime was 10 o'clock sharp, but Poe often broke the rules and went drinking instead.[19] The discipline of West Point was hard for Poe. He only wanted to write, but realized he needed to provide financially for himself. Just as he had in the Army, Poe soon wanted out of West Point.

Poe attended the Army's West Point military academy.

Famous West Point Graduates

Edgar Allan Poe was just one in a long line of famous students who have attended school at West Point since it opened in 1802. Poe did not graduate from the school, but some noteworthy people did, including:[20]

- U.S. President Ulysses S. Grant
- U.S. President Dwight D. Eisenhower
- Astronaut Edwin E. "Buzz" Aldrin, the second man to walk on the moon
- Army generals George S. Patton and Douglas MacArthur
- Confederate Army general Robert E. Lee
- Mike "Coach K" Krzyzewski, famous college basketball and United States Olympic basketball team coach

Poe's good relationship with his foster father, regained after the death of his foster mother, did not stay that way for long. John Allan remarried after Fanny's death. Soon, he and his foster son were again quarreling. But Poe still needed Allan's help. This time it was to get paid when he left West Point. To get his money, Poe needed his guardian's permission to resign. So he wrote another letter. In the letter, he talked about how Allan had taken him in as a young child and promised to help him out. Poe said that obligation had not been honored. Poe, sick at the time, also wrote,

"If I do not receive your answer in 10 days, I will leave . . ."[21] Allan never responded. Poe began skipping classes and neglecting his other duties. He was dismissed from the school in early 1831. Broke again, this time he moved to New York City.

Struggling Writer

No one knows how Poe spent his first few weeks in New York. But through his works, they know he kept writing. In May 1831, *Poems* was published. The small book was dedicated to Poe's former classmates at West Point. The classmates had paid for the book's publication. It contained several reprinted versions of poems from his previous book. There were also some unpublished poems, including "To Helen," which he had written years ago about Jane Stanard, the now-dead mother of his childhood friend.

Poe did not receive much pay or recognition for his third book. A couple of newspapers wrote small articles about it. The West Point cadets the book was dedicated to did not like it. In general, they received it with a lot of "disgust."[22] It was very different from Poe's other writings that the cadets had liked.

Poe soon moved back to Baltimore, then the second-largest city in the United States. There, he stayed with the family of his birth father. The group lived in a house with several people, including his grandmother; his brother, William Henry; his young cousin, Virginia; and his aunt, Maria Clemm, whom he called "Muddy." Clemm was the sister of Poe's missing father, and a widow. Some of the people in the crowded house were in poor health. Poe's grandmother was bedridden. Poe said his brother was "slowly dying of tuberculosis and alcoholism."[23] Though they were all poor, Clemm managed to keep the house together. And, somehow, Poe continued writing.

In 1832, the *Philadelphia Saturday Courier* published five of his short stories. He still did not get any money for them. Poe was now twenty-three years old. He had published three books and several articles but was not making money writing. He could not help but wonder: Was his foster father right? Was there no money to be made as a writer? Soon, Poe would have his answer.

Maria "Muddy" Clemm would become very close with her nephew, Edgar Allan Poe.

In June 1833, he entered a few of his short stories in a contest. The first prize was fifty dollars. Three months later, Poe's short story, "MS. Found in a Bottle," was announced as the winner. The money certainly was helpful to his poor household. The publicity and connections Poe gained were equally helpful. Poe finally made money doing what he always wanted to do, and what his foster father thought would never happen. He now felt more strongly—and had proof—he could earn a living as a writer.

5

Writing to Live

Poe appeared headed for happiness after he won the writing contest. But his life had never been easy or simple. It was not this time, either. The good news of winning the grand prize of fifty dollars was followed by bad news. Now remarried with three young children, John Allan had fallen ill. Poe's hot, cold, and oftentimes absent relationship with his foster father was nearing its tragic end. Some say Poe made one final visit to Allan in Richmond.

As that story goes, Poe knocked on the door of Allan's huge home and was told he could not come in. He came through the door anyway and went upstairs to Allan's room, where the ill man lied in bed. According to historian Arthur Hobson Quinn, ". . . Mr. Allan raised his cane, and threatening to strike him if he came within his reach, ordered him out . . ."[1] Poe left and the two men never saw each other again. John Allan died on March 27, 1834. He was fifty-four, and Poe was twenty-five.

Others doubt Poe's visit to John Allan's deathbed happened. They believe it is just another fictitious part of Poe's often-exaggerated legend. Regardless, Poe was not in Allan's will. He received nothing from his foster father's vast fortune. It was always in the back of Poe's mind that he would get a lot of money when Allan died. Knowing that allowed him more freedom to take chances with his writing, and life in general, because he thought he would inherit enough to live on.

Because that did not happen, Poe had to continue finding a way to earn a living on his own. He wanted to contribute to his household. He was still living in poverty at his aunt Muddy Clemm's house. The only three people left there were his sick grandmother, Clemm, and her twelve-year-old daughter, Virginia. Poe's brother, William Henry, had died in 1831.

The Magazine Business

The judges of the writing contest Poe had won helped him in many ways. One judge, John Pendleton

The Popularity of Magazines

The word "magazine" comes from the Arabic word "makhazin," meaning "storehouses." The first-known magazine, *The Gentleman's Magazine*, was published in 1731 in London. The first magazine in the United States was published ten years later. Magazine production soared during Edgar Allan Poe's lifetime as more people learned how to read. Other forms of entertainment—such as television, radio, and computers—were still decades from existence.

Kennedy, told Poe about a new magazine in Richmond, Virginia. It was called the *Southern Literary Messenger*. Soon, Poe had several of his stories published in the magazine. More importantly, he was getting paid for them. He also wrote book reviews for the *Messenger*. In 1835, he became the owner's assistant. He basically was the magazine's editor, but the owner did not call him that because he wanted it to look like he was still in control. Poe's salary began at fifteen dollars a week. He had to move 150 miles back to Richmond to earn it.

A Controversial Marriage

Many people have tried to guess what Poe was thinking when he made the next big move in his personal life.

He may have done it solely out of love. He may have done it for security, because he did not want to be alone anymore. He may have done it out of jealousy, or so his latest mother figure, Aunt Muddy Clemm, would always be around to care for him. Whatever the reason, Poe began to pursue romantically his thirteen-year-old cousin, Virginia. He was not keeping it secret.

Poe sent a letter from Richmond to Baltimore confessing to Clemm his love for Virginia. The letter said, "I am blinded with tears while writing this letter—I have no wish to live another hour."[2] He wrote the letter after learning a relative, Neilson Poe, had offered to take care of Virginia to provide the poor girl with an education. If that happened, Poe knew he probably would never see her again. He would also never again see Clemm, because she would stay in Baltimore, too. Two more females Poe was close to, like his birth mother, foster mother, and others, would be gone from his life forever.

Poe's letter continued. He asked Clemm, "Do you think any one could love her more dearly than I? . . . Kiss her for me—a million times."[3] To Virginia, Poe wrote, "My love, my own sweetest Sissy, my darling little wifey, think well before you break the heart of your cousin Eddy."[4] Poe enclosed five dollars to help pay for their needs. He hoped it would help. He soon decided he needed to do something more drastic to ensure they would choose to move to Richmond. He abruptly left his job and rushed to Baltimore. When he arrived, he asked Clemm if he could marry Virginia. Clemm agreed, but only if Poe could get his job back.

There is no known photograph of Virginia Poe. This watercolor was painted in 1847.

Poe was willing to do whatever it took and asked his boss. The boss agreed to hire him back under certain conditions. He was afraid Poe's drinking would return. The boss wrote, ". . . I have my fears . . . that you would again sip the juice. No man is safe who drinks before breakfast. No man can do so, and attend to business properly."[5] Poe promised not to drink and returned to Richmond with Clemm and Virginia. During the fall of 1835, Poe and Virginia got a marriage license. Virginia was thirteen. Poe was twice her age. Some historians believe the couple secretly married at this time, as well, but little evidence has been found to back up that theory. The public wedding ceremony did not take place until the following spring, on May 16, 1836.

Nowadays, Poe's marriage might seem strange for many reasons. First, marrying your first cousin is illegal in more than half of the United States. But many states, and other countries, still allow it. In Poe's time, marrying your first cousin was not uncommon. There were said to be benefits to marrying someone familiar instead of someone who was almost a stranger. It was thought to help your family prosper by keeping money and workers in the family.

However, an adult marrying a thirteen-year-old child is not accepted in society today. The state of New Hampshire allows a girl that young to marry, but she can only do so with permission of her parents and a judge. Even in Poe's day, marrying someone that young was not normal. Society likely frowned upon it, because the marriage certificate claimed Virginia was twenty-one years old.[6] Yet the two cousins wed, and Virginia Clemm became Virginia Poe. Each day, the young bride stayed at home and continued her schooling while her new husband went to work.

Locks of Edgar Allan Poe's (right) and Virginia Poe's hair were taken after their deaths and pressed under glass. Poe's family kept them as mementos, which was the custom at the time. Today, the locks are housed at the Enoch Pratt Free Library in Baltimore.

A Harsh Critic

The *Southern Literary Messenger* blossomed under Poe's leadership. It became well respected. Poe's writings became popular. Subscriptions to the magazine soared. But working at the magazine took time away from Poe's dream. He was working for someone else. What he really wanted was to be his own boss.

For this and other reasons, Poe grew unhappy and began writing less for the *Messenger*. At the same time, Poe also became known for being coldhearted when reviewing other people's books, short stories, and poetry. He had the reputation of being a harsh critic. Poe's boss took a lot of heat for that and was growing tired of it. Poe later said he did not make enough money, and that is why he quit working there in January 1837. No one knows what really led to his departure. Was it because he was unhappy? Was it because his boss was unhappy? Readers were simply told Poe was ". . . bidding all parties a peaceable farewell."[7]

Moving Around

Poe, Virginia, and Clemm left Richmond and returned to New York City. In the much-bigger metropolis, Poe found a publisher for his story *The Narrative of Arthur Gordon Pym*. The book was published in 1838. The fictional plot was a twisted tale revolving around the title character, who hides out on a whaling ship. The ship sets sail and wrecks. Many weird situations follow, and there is a mysterious ending. Poe made the book

An Interview With a Poe

Imagine what it is like being related to a man as legendary as Edgar Allan Poe. Dr. Harry L. Poe is. A professor at Union University in Jackson, Tennessee, and also an author, Dr. Poe says his last name is recognized everywhere he goes. People always want to know if he is related to Edgar. He answered some questions about what it is like to be a Poe.

Q: How are you related to Edgar Allan Poe?

A: Edgar Allan Poe was the cousin of my great-great-grandfather, William Poe.[8]

Q: Do you have any interesting stories about being related to Edgar Allan Poe?

A: I just returned from Cancún [Mexico] where the receptionist at the hotel immediately asked if I was related to Poe. This happens all over the world. People everywhere know his name. The clerks who take my credit card at stores, gas stations, and hotels will regularly quote a few lines from "The Raven" or "Annabel Lee."[9]

Q: When did you first become aware your last name had special significance?

A: I have always been aware of Poe. When I was a small child, before beginning school, we visited the Charleston [South Carolina] Museum, which had a shadow box of Poe on Sullivan's Island where he set "The Gold-Bug." My grandfather had a letter from Poe that had been handed down from his grandfather, William.[10]

Q: Which are your favorite of your cousin's works and why?

A: My favorite story is probably the "The Cask of Amontillado" because it explores how sin turns us into monsters by nurturing grudges.[11]

so lifelike many thought it was a true story. Partially because people were confused as to what type of writing it was, the story was not well received. Today, people understand it is fiction and consider it a classic.

The family did not stay long in New York before moving to Philadelphia. The Pennsylvania city is nick-named the "City of Brotherly Love." It turned out to be very loving to Poe, but not at first. Philadelphia offered many outlets for a writer to publish his work. While Virginia went to school and Clemm tended to the house, Poe wrote. His income was not steady, but he did manage to publish writings and make a little money doing so.

Creepy Tales

Steady work finally came again in 1839, when William Evans Burton hired Poe as an editorial assistant for *Burton's Gentleman's Magazine*. Poe had many duties there, including reviewing other writers' works, which had gotten him into some trouble at his previous job. Also similar to his previous job, he was publishing his own writings in this magazine. Two of his most famous fiction stories were published in *Burton's*—"The Fall of the House of Usher" and "William Wilson."

"The Fall of the House of Usher" is a spooky tale about a brother and sister living in a creepy mansion. Both siblings soon experience mysterious health problems.

Many of the writing characteristics Poe is now famous for are present in "The Fall of the House of

BURTON'S

GENTLEMAN'S MAGAZINE.

EDITED BY

WILLIAM E. BURTON AND EDGAR A. POE.

VOLUME V.

FROM JULY TO DECEMBER.

By a gentleman, we mean not to draw a line that would be invidious between high and low, rank and subordination, riches and poverty. No. *The distinction is in the mind.* Whoever is open, just, and true; whoever is of a humane and affable demeanor; whoever is honorable in himself, and in his judgment of others, and requires no law but his word to make him fulfil an engagement;—such a man is a gentleman;—and such a man may be found among the tillers of the earth as well as in the drawing rooms of the high born and the rich.

DE VERE.

PHILADELPHIA.
PUBLISHED BY WILLIAM E. BURTON,
DOCK STREET, OPPOSITE THE EXCHANGE.

1839.

Poe was listed as an editor on the cover of this July 1829 edition of Burton's Gentleman's Magazine.

Usher." The mood of the story is gothic, or eerie and gloomy, and there is a frightful ending. The story is full of symbolism, or using one object to represent another. For example, to most, the story's setting would just be a house. But Poe makes it frightening, and gives it characteristics of a human face:

> *I looked upon the scene before me—upon the mere house, and the simple landscape features of the domain—upon the bleak walls—upon the vacant eye-like windows—upon a few rank sedges—and upon a few white trunks of decayed trees—with an utter depression of soul which I can compare to no earthly sensation more properly than to the after-dream of the reveler upon opium—the bitter lapse into every-day life—the hideous dropping off of the veil. There was an iciness, a sinking, a sickening of the heart . . .*[12]

"William Wilson" is also spooky and strange. The plot features the narrator, William Wilson, who had been a student in a schoolhouse resembling the building in "The Fall of the House of Usher." William Wilson, the narrator, soon meets another student named William Wilson who looks and acts a lot like him. He even starts to copy him. A rivalry between the two boys begins. They eventually fight, and the narrator moves away. But the second William Wilson shows up wherever the narrator goes:

> *Upon my entering he strode hurriedly up to me, and, seizing me by the arm with a gesture of*

Mr. Wilson meets his double in this illustration from the story
"William Wilson," by Edgar Allan Poe.

petulant impatience, whispered the words "William Wilson!" in my ear.[13]

At the end of the story, the reader is left wondering: Was the second William Wilson real or imaginary? The second William Wilson was a doppelganger, a living person's ghostly double. Poe's use of the doppelganger allows him to show a character's alter ego.

As excellent and respected as his work was becoming, Poe still found himself in debt. He was not making enough money from his writings. His extra work outside of *Burton's* did not help much. Even his publishing of *Tales of the Grotesque and Arabesque* did not help. That book featured twenty-five stories, but Poe's only payment was a few copies.

Poe was still unsatisfied with the direction his career was going. After a year, the working relationship between Poe and Burton ended. Burton wrote in a letter that he fired Poe. Poe wrote in a letter that he quit. Whatever the reason was, dreams of becoming his own boss obviously were on Poe's mind. Now, he wanted to start his own magazine.

Quoth the Raven

I t costs a lot of money to run a magazine. Starting one from scratch is even more expensive. But that is what Poe wanted to do. Because he did not have much money, he asked for help. First, he created a prospectus, which is a written plan that lets people know what the business will be about in hopes they will invest money in it. Poe's prospectus included the name of his publication, which he planned to call *Penn Magazine*. He said it would publish once a month and cost five dollars a year to subscribe. The first issue was scheduled to come out on January 1, 1841. But the money never came in as he had hoped, so Poe postponed the starting date. He promised he would start it again sometime later. He never did.

A New Type of Story

Needing to support Muddy Clemm and Virginia Poe, Poe returned to work for someone else. This time it was *Graham's Magazine*. Poe became the editor there, and the owner even promised to one day help him start his own magazine.[1] Poe believed he was on the right track.

One of the first of his own writings Poe printed in the magazine was called "The Murders in the Rue Morgue." The fictional tale is believed to be the first-ever detective story. In it, Poe introduced a character named C. Auguste Dupin. In the story, set in Paris, everyone believed it was impossible to solve the brutal killings of two people. The story's narrator said, "I could merely agree with all Paris in considering them an insoluble mystery. I saw no means by which it would be possible to trace the murderer."[2] However, Dupin figured it out. The Dupin character later appeared in two of Poe's other detective stories, "The Mystery of Marie Roget" and "The Purloined Letter."

Graham's Magazine prospered under Poe's direction, as had *Burton's* and the *Southern Literary Messenger* before it. When Poe began reviewing and writing for *Graham's*, roughly five thousand people subscribed. At the end of his first year on the job, eight times that many did. The magazine also increased in size. The quality of the writing grew, as well.

After work each day, Poe continued writing on his own time. By all accounts, his drinking did not appear to be a problem during this time. All seemed well, but it never stayed that way for long during Poe's troubled life. Some believed his life was cursed; most thought it was his own doing. Poe was a hard person to keep happy and was often confrontational. It is not clear which one, if either, of those characteristics led to Poe's departure from *Graham's*. But, after working there a little more than a year and achieving many successes, he quit. Poe wrote, "My reason for resigning was disgust with the namby-pamby character of the Magazine . . . I allude to the contemptible pictures, fashion-plates, music, and love-tales. The salary, moreover, did not pay me for the labour which I was forced to bestow."[3] Poe had high standards when writing was concerned. He knew what he wanted out of a magazine. *Graham's* was not giving it to him.

> "My reason for resigning was disgust with the namby-pamby character of the Magazine . . ."

Terrible News

The one aspect of Poe's life he was nearly always pleased with, at least since his marriage to Virginia, was his personal life. At home, he drew comfort from his motherly aunt, Muddy Clemm, and the young wife he had grown to love so dearly. However, problems started to occur at home, as well. The biggest one was out of Poe's control. It began a short time before he resigned from *Graham's*.

Virginia Poe had become a good pianist and loved to sing. In January 1842, she started to bleed from the mouth while at home singing and playing the piano. Historians now know it was because she had tuberculosis, the same disease that had killed Poe's mother. Like Eliza Poe, Virginia was also young when she was stricken. She was also never the same. Neither was Poe, who cared deeply for his wife.[4]

Problems With Alcohol

Writers such as William Faulkner, Ernest Hemingway, and, most recently, horror writer Stephen King all had problems with alcohol. Alcohol can be addictive and frequently causes problems of its own. Any issues the user might think alcohol temporarily numbs are often replaced with problems that are far worse. If Poe knew this, it did not deter him. He still used alcohol throughout life to deal with depression and stress. As a short, slender man, even little amounts would impair him greatly. Poe drank heavily after Virginia became ill. He later wrote, ". . . I drank, God only knows how often

> "[Drinking] has been the desperate attempt to escape from torturing memories"

or how much."[5] He also said, "[Drinking] has been the desperate attempt to escape from torturing memories, from a sense of insupportable loneliness, and a dread of some strange impending doom."[6]

Tales of Terror

Another way many cope with stress is by working a lot. Poe did this, too. His writing, along with alcohol, offered him an escape from his life. Many of his best known stories were written during this time, including "The Pit and the Pendulum." The horror story is about a prisoner who is sentenced to death. The man is first strapped to a table with a giant blade swinging over him. Panic takes hold as the blade, ever so slowly, moves closer:

> *Down—still unceasingly—still inevitably down! I gasped and struggled at each vibration. I shrunk convulsively at its every sweep. My eyes followed its outward or upward whirls with the eagerness of the most unmeaning despair; they closed themselves spasmodically at the descent, although death would have been a relief, oh! how unspeakable!*[7]

Just before the blade slices him, the man escapes. But then he finds the walls of his room beginning to close. Eventually, the walls push him toward a pit in the middle of the room. The story then comes to an exciting end. Many cartoons and movies have used Poe's ideas from that story for their own.

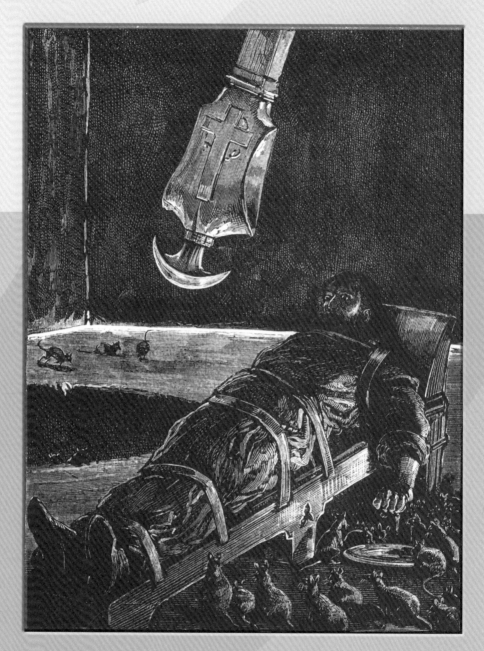

A prisoner condemned to death looks up at a razor-sharp pendulum blade as rats get ready to chew through the ropes that bind him. This illustration from "The Pit and the Pendulum" was published in London, England, in 1882.

Poe also wrote an equally disturbing story, "The Tell-Tale Heart," during this time. The story's plot features a narrator who murders a man and hides his body under the floor. When police arrive, the subject imagines he hears the murdered man's heart, which keeps growing louder:

> *I paced the floor to and fro with heavy strides, as if excited to fury by the observations of the men—but the noise steadily increased. Oh God! what could I do? I foamed—I raved—I swore! I swung the chair upon which I had been sitting, and grated it upon the boards, but the noise arose over all and continually increased. It grew louder—louder—louder!*[8]

"The Tell-Tale Heart" is an excellent example of Poe's use of an unreliable narrator. Poe often used the literary device, in which the tellers of his tales are not as credible as normal narrators. Oftentimes, it is because they are somewhat insane. The unreliable narrator often leaves questions in the reader's mind: What was real? What was not?

Realistic Writing

Both "The Pit and the Pendulum," which originally appeared in an anthology, and "The Tell-Tale Heart" were published in magazines. So was "The Gold-Bug," which earned Poe a hundred-dollar prize from a Philadelphia newspaper in June 1843. The story was set on Sullivan's Island, the place where Poe had lived while in the Army.

His writings continued doing well. But Poe still longed to start a magazine of his own. While Muddy Clemm stayed in Philadelphia, Poe and his ill wife, Virginia, moved back to New York in early 1844. In April, Poe wrote a newspaper article for the New York *Sun*. The article is now known as "The Balloon-Hoax." It told a highly detailed story of a man flying a balloon across the Atlantic Ocean. This had never been done before. When Poe told the story, he said a large crowd surrounded the newspaper office, anxious to get a copy of the article. It was the talk of the town. People were paying great amounts of money for a copy. Everyone thought Poe was publicizing an historical event, and they all wanted to have a keepsake of it. The paper it was in sold about fifty thousand copies.[9]

> **"I never witnessed more intense excitement to get possession of a newspaper."**

The truth was, the story was not real. Once again, it all had come from Poe's imagination. But many believed it, just like they believed *The Narrative of Arthur Gordon Pym* years earlier. Poe said later, "I never witnessed more intense excitement to get possession of a newspaper. As soon as the first few copies made their way into the streets, they were bought up, almost at any price . . ."[10] People were not happy when the story later was revealed to be untrue. But it did show the power of Poe's storytelling. He was a master. The first balloon with a human aboard did not cross the Atlantic until 1978, 134 years after Poe had written about it.

A Literary Feud

In May 1844, Clemm finally left Philadelphia to come to New York to join Edgar Allan and Virginia Poe. In June, the three of them moved outside the city to an enormous farm owned by the Brennan family. Again with a full family—including a sick wife—to support, it was more important for Poe to have a steady job. He found one at the New York *Evening Mirror* newspaper. It paid him fifteen dollars a week. The job was not as glamorous as some he had before. But Poe had to take it to pay for his family's survival.

Needless to say, Poe was still unhappy. A feud began between him and another American writer, Henry Wadsworth Longfellow. Poe had once written how he was positively affected by Longfellow's good work. He wrote, ". . . all that I have read from your pen has inspired me with a high idea of your power; and I think you are destined to stand among the first romance writers of our country . . ."[11]

But Longfellow was also a poet. His work was more popular with the public than Poe's, which was not always as uplifting. Longfellow was also far richer. Some historians believe Poe became jealous of Longfellow. He wrote many negative reviews about Longfellow's writing. He even accused him of plagiarism, or stealing someone else's writing and calling it one's own.

Popular Poem

Poe did not have to be jealous of Longfellow long because his life changed dramatically, beginning

January 29, 1845. That is when the *Evening Mirror* published "The Raven." There is some debate as to whether the *Evening Mirror* was the first to publish the poem. *The American Review* magazine ran it in its February issue, and magazines often come out prior to their dates. Regardless, "The Raven" is about a man whose wife had died. Nearly asleep, the narrator is startled awake by a knock at the door. The knocking continues, and he finally opens his window and sees a black raven sitting there. He speaks to the bird. The only word the bird says is "Nevermore," as the man grows more and more frustrated pondering what the bird means.

Today, even the most excellent poems regularly go unnoticed. But, in Poe's time, reading was a top source of recreation and communication. If people wanted to talk to someone far away, they did not pick up the phone. They did not send an e-mail or an instant message. They mailed a letter. If people wanted the news, they did not watch TV or log on to the Internet. They read a newspaper. So when more newspapers across the country wrote about or reprinted "The Raven," it became immensely popular. Soon, everyone was talking about it. People were going around repeating, "Nevermore."[12] The poem was mysterious. Tension and drama continually build from the opening line on. People wanted to know everything about the man whose brilliant mind could create such a masterpiece.

Three of the poem's main themes—lost love, death, and loneliness—are found throughout many of Poe's works. The fact is not surprising. Poe regularly wrote about his personal experiences.

"The Raven" made Poe famous almost overnight. For years he had toiled between poverty and desperation, but soon everyone knew him. The poem was a smash and received many favorable reviews. Other writers imitated it and changed the words for their own stories. In those days, what copyright laws there were did little to protect authors. People could take a writer's work and reprint it as many times as they wanted without paying to do it. So Poe got little money for writing the poem that made him a household name. Estimates of his pay range from nine to thirty dollars. Today, many still consider it the most popular poem in American history. People have made money using its theme in TV shows, reprinting the poem in other publications, and even reciting it in plays. But back then, all it did for Poe financially was give him a few more dollars.

Three of the poem's main themes—lost love, death, and loneliness—are found throughout many of Poe's works.

Writing "The Raven" may not have made Poe rich, but it did place his writings in high demand. It also helped him meet a lot of important people. Poe soon left the *Evening Mirror* to work at the *Broadway Journal*. The *Journal* was a new magazine and Poe was named coeditor. He was also given part ownership of the magazine.

Mr HENRY LUDLOWE
in
THE RAVEN
THE LOVE STORY OF EDGAR ALLAN POE
DIRECTION
HAZELTON & NORTH   BY GEORGE HAZELTON

"The Raven" has continued to be popular long after Poe's death. This poster advertises an early twentieth-century play based on the poem.

A Failed Reading

Poe was being asked to speak in public and getting paid for it. He recited his poetry almost like a song. His appearances were well attended and received good reviews. However, he made people upset during one speech. Poe had traveled to Boston to speak to a large crowd and was paid fifty dollars. After he finished, most crowd members did not think he earned his money. Poe bored everyone with a long, older poem, "Al-Aaraaf," that many did not understand. He was supposed to read a new poem but could not come up with one in time. Poe finally read "The Raven" at the end of his speech. But by then, most of the crowd had left. Papers wrote about how the performance bombed.

Poe said he acted the way he did to rebel. Often when a musician, writer, or another type of artist becomes popular, people who do not understand their art begin to follow them because it is the "in" thing to do. Poe believed many people in the crowd were only there because he was popular, not because they liked his poetry. He also thought the audience was snooty and that he was not paid enough for his time. Poe wrote about the event later. He wrote the poem he read was, ". . . the best we had—for the price . . ."[13]

Getting Paid

"The Raven" continued to help fuel Poe's popularity in 1845. Because of the poem's success, he was able to publish two books that year. The first was called *Tales* and was published in June. It included twelve previously published short stories. The book sold for fifty cents and Poe received eight cents from each copy sold.[14]

The Raven and Other Poems was also published in 1845. That book contained thirty of Poe's best poems, including "The Raven," which was the book's first poem. Several of the other poems were reprinted from his second book, *Al Aaraaf, Tamerlane and Other Minor Poems.* Those poems were more than fourteen years old. Poe was paid a total of seventy-five dollars for *The Raven and Other Poems.*[15] The book sold for thirty-one cents a copy.

Meanwhile, Poe stayed with his job at the *Broadway Journal.* Despite his problems in Boston, his return to New York City worked out well. He was offered an opportunity to take over the *Broadway Journal* by himself. For just fifty dollars—the amount he was paid for his disappointing Boston speech—he could own the magazine. Poe no longer had the fifty dollars but found someone to loan it to him. In October 1845, after all his years of dreams, Poe finally owned his own magazine. Now he could do things his own way. Finally, he was in charge.

Rough Times

Poe's magazine was not in good financial shape when he inherited it. He had to borrow money to buy the *Broadway Journal*; now he had to borrow more to keep it going. Under these circumstances, the magazine did not last long. Its last issue came out in January 1846. In it, Poe wrote, ". . . I now, as its Editor, bid farewell . . ."[1]

Poe only had his dream in his hands for two months. During that time, he saw the magazine continue to fail. He became depressed, and again began drinking heavily. Owning a magazine turned out to be another disappointment. Poe was having a hard time dealing with it.

Fighting Illness

With failure fresh on his mind, Poe moved his family a couple of times before settling in a quiet neighborhood named Fordham in The Bronx, a section of New York City. There, Poe rented a small house for one hundred dollars a year.[2] The house, built in 1812, had five small rooms, including two tiny ones in the attic. There may not have been much space but the quiet location was a perfect place for Virginia Poe, growing sicker from tuberculosis, to rest.

Edgar Allan Poe himself had become ill with an unknown condition. Historians now believe it was depression, which is a reason many turn to alcohol. After he had given the disappointing speech in Boston, his reputation began to slide back downhill. Then he started drinking again. Then his magazine failed. And his wife was still sick. The media even began publicizing his predicament. One newspaper wrote, ". . . Mr. Edgar A. Poe, the poet and author, has been deranged, and his friends are about to place him under the charge of Dr. Brigham, of the Insane Retreat at Utica."[3] Poe was never put in a mental hospital, nor was he close to going there. It turned out to be a rumor, but people who read it believed it. All the negative events in Poe's life contributed to his depression. A visit from his sister,

The house where Poe lived in The Bronx, New York, is a museum today. It is called Poe Cottage.

Rosalie, whom he had not seen for a long while, did not cheer him up.

Inciting Anger

Poe was having trouble doing what he loved most—writing. Writing letters was even hard for him. He did manage some reviews of others' works. For a few months in the middle of 1846, Poe's "The Literati of New York City" was published in *Godey's Lady's Book* magazine. "The Literati" contained short biographies and critiques of then-popular writers and editors. Reviewers are supposed to give their honest opinions of work they read. They are not always nice with their comments. Poe was not either, but his reviews were often personal. Many of those reviewed became angry at his words.

At the end of each person's mention, Poe wrote a paragraph describing the looks of the author he was writing about. Today, pictures would be used instead, but then, photographs were rare and expensive. So, many reviewers described authors with words. Poe often was not nice with his descriptions. He said one man's face was "strongly pitted by the small-pox."[4] He even attacked people who once were his friends. It would have been interesting to read how Poe would have described his own physical attributes. His cute boyhood features had changed. His large forehead, dark eyes, and dark hair, in particular, have since become a prototype for creepy characters on TV and in movies.

One positive in Poe's depressed life was the ability to spend more time with his sick wife. He rarely left home and felt guilty when he did. Once, when he had to stay elsewhere overnight, he wrote to his wife, "You are my *greatest* and *only* stimulus now, to battle with this uncongenial, unsatisfactory, and ungrateful life."[5] The words show he clearly cared for Virginia. They also show Poe was unhappy with what his life had become.

A Husband's Loss

Newspaper and magazine notices continued to inform people that Poe and his wife were not doing well. One reporter wrote Poe was "dangerously ill with the brain fever"[6] and Virginia was "in the last stages"[7] of living.

It said they ". . . are without money and without friends . . ."[8] The articles let the public know the couple needed support. It was the same thing that happened with Poe's mother years earlier when Poe was a child. When his mother became sick, people began giving her charity. Poe and his wife were now in the same situation.

> One reporter wrote Poe was "dangerously ill with the brain fever."

A friend who helped care for Virginia Poe wrote about what her life was like in the Fordham house. She said, "She lay on the straw bed, wrapped in her husband's great-coat, with a large tortoise-shell cat on her bosom . . . The coat and the cat were [Virginia's] only means of warmth, except as her husband held her hands, and her mother her feet."[9]

Virginia ultimately had two final, miserable traits in common with the mother-in-law she never knew. On January 30, 1847, Virginia died of tuberculosis, the same disease that had killed Eliza Poe. Also like Eliza Poe, she was twenty-four years old when she died.

A Collapse

Poe had just turned thirty-eight when he collapsed from stress and exhaustion following Virginia's death. Muddy Clemm helped care for him. She had promised her daughter she would. On February 17, Poe won more than $225 in a lawsuit against the owners of the New York *Evening Mirror*. It was the newspaper where he used to work, and the one that had helped him achieve major success by publishing "The Raven." Poe's lawsuit claimed the owners had published an article that libeled him, or damaged his reputation.

Clemm was sent to pick up the money. Poe had not even shown for the trial. He stayed home most of the time in 1847, either physically sick, mentally depressed, or both. When he did leave home, he was quick to return to its comforts. The lawsuit money was basically all he and Muddy had to live on the entire year. Clemm tried to sell some of Poe's writings to magazines but had little, if any, success.

Whatever Poe did, most likely rest and reclusion, to regain his health took a long time. But it seemed to work. By early 1848, Poe decided he wanted to get back to work. Magazines wrote about his triumphant return. Poe decided to mostly focus on starting his own magazine. For the rest of his life, this would be his main purpose.

Back to Work

Poe traveled again and gave lectures in various cities. He wrote one of his best poems, "Ulalume." Not surprisingly, it was about a man who had lost the woman he loved. It was set in a forest by a lake. Poe's writings were often inspired by his life. The story of "Ulalume" resembled Poe's situation. Most people believe Virginia inspired it. As it was in "The Raven," the theme of death is prevalent:

> *Thus I pacified Psyche and kissed her,*
> *And tempted her out of her gloom—*

And conquered her scruples and gloom;
And we passed to the end of a vista,
But were stopped by the door of a tomb—
By the door of a legended tomb;

And I said—"What is written, sweet sister,
On the door of this legended tomb?"
She replied—"Ulalume—Ulalume—
'Tis the vault of thy lost Ulalume!"[10]

In 1848, Poe also published *Eureka*. The essay was different from his usual writings. *Eureka* was Poe's explanation of the universe. Reviews of *Eureka* were mixed. People either loved it or hated it. Today, when people talk about Poe's writings, they often overlook *Eureka*. It does not fit into the categories of work he was best known for—short stories and poems.

Poe spent most of the first year and a half after Virginia's death sick and grieving over the woman he loved so dearly—the one who called him "Eddy,"—the one who was his "Sissy." In the summer of 1848, he appeared ready to try and begin a new long-term relationship. Poe knew a few women in

> Poe spent most of the first year and a half after Virginia's death sick and grieving over the woman he loved so dearly.

different states he had met through his travels. On a trip to Richmond, he even considered getting engaged again to Elmira Royster, whose father had broken up the relationship years earlier when both were young.

New Love

One significant new romance in Poe's life was with a woman from Rhode Island. Her name was Sarah Helen Whitman, but she went by her middle name of Helen. Whitman had fallen in love with Poe's writing several years before and had tried to make contact with him for a while. Poe soon wrote a new poem to her called "To Helen." He had written a different poem by the same name years before. When he once saw her long ago, Poe wrote in the newer poem, nothing else in the world existed:

> And in an instant all things disappeared.
> (Ah, bear in mind this garden was enchanted!)
> The pearly lustre of the moon went out:
> The mossy banks and the meandering paths,
> The happy flowers and the repining trees,
> Were seen no more: the very roses' odors
> Died in the arms of the adoring airs.
> All—all expired save thee—save less than thou:
> Save only the divine light in thine eyes—
> Save but the soul in thine uplifted eyes.
> I saw but them—they were the world to me.
> I saw but them—saw only them for hours—
> Saw only them until the moon went down.[11]

Poe and Whitman finally met in person in September 1848. Whitman was a few years older than Poe. Her husband had died several years before. After a couple of days together, Poe asked Whitman to marry him. She said she needed to think about it, and Poe returned home to New York City.

For several reasons, Whitman decided not to marry Poe. The determined Poe kept asking anyway, and became upset at receiving the same negative answer.

Poe began drinking more. It was clear Poe probably would not make a good husband. So it was odd when Whitman finally agreed to marry Poe; many people had warned her not to. It was most likely because she wanted to help the talented man who was in such bad shape. Like he had before for other people who had asked him to, Poe agreed to quit drinking.

But Poe's wild ways eventually became too much for even the loving Whitman. He did not quit drinking, so she decided to break off the engagement. Another reason was that Whitman's mother believed Poe only wanted to get married because he was poor and her family was rich. The broken engagement was another horrible blow to Poe. Again, depression followed.

Poe fell in love with Sarah Helen Whitman about a year and a half after his wife's death.

A Married Woman

Poe's writing was nowhere near as high profile as it had been immediately following "The Raven." Many people had forgotten about him. Based on newspaper reports and his lengthy absence, others thought he was dead. But Poe was still publishing some excellent work and lecturing. In many places, he was still popular. In fact, almost two thousand people showed up at one of his speeches in late 1848.

His career, and thoughts of his own magazine, remained important. Romance was also at the front of Poe's mind. Even as he was preparing to marry Whitman, Poe had strong feelings for a woman from Massachusetts. Her name was Nancy Richmond. For whatever reason, Poe called her "Annie."

One day during this period, Poe decided to take a drug called laudanum. Laudanum was a mixture of alcohol and opium, which comes from a poppy plant. Today, drug users often take heroin, which also comes from the poppy plant. Both laudanum and heroin are illegal, dangerous, and highly addictive. It is easy to overdose and die from them. Most historians believe Poe was so depressed that he could not be with Annie Richmond that he was trying to kill himself. As evidence, they cite a letter Poe wrote to Richmond: ". . . I feel I CANNOT live, unless

> "I feel I CANNOT live, unless I can feel your sweet, gentle, loving hand pressed upon my forehead . . ."

I can feel your sweet, gentle, loving hand pressed upon my forehead . . ."[12]

The drug made Poe very sick. He was not the healthiest individual anyway, and taking drugs certainly did not help him.

To complicate matters, Richmond was married. But Poe was invited to stay with her and her husband anyway while he visited the couple's town. It was a strange situation, and Richmond's husband even allowed Poe to hold his wife's hand. Some say it is because the husband thought the relationship was more like a brother and sister than lovers. He was not jealous of Poe. He thought Poe was harmless. Poe wrote a poem about this love interest, as well. He called it, "For Annie."

> *But my heart it is brighter*
> *Than all of the many*
> *Stars in the sky,*
> *For it sparkles with Annie—*
> *It glows with the light*
> *Of the love of my Annie—*
> *With the thought of the light*
> *Of the eyes of my Annie.*[13]

To many, it was clear. Poe thought of Annie as more than a sister. Eventually, her husband became suspicious of Poe's motives.

Chapter

8

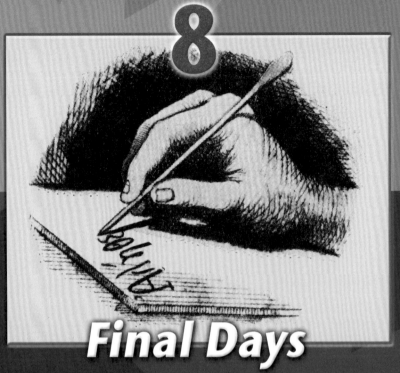

Final Days

Regardless of what Poe wanted out of it, the relationship with Annie Richmond did not work. Given the fact that she was married, it should not have come as a surprise. But Poe had poured his heart into loving her. He wrote, ". . . [love] burns in my very soul for *you*—so pure—so unworldly—a love which would make *all* sacrifices for your sake."[1] Yet it was another romantic disappointment for Poe.

His writing career again had become a disappointment, as well. He was not publishing many works. He was writing steadily for a small magazine called *The Flag of Our Union*, mostly because he needed the money. Writing poetry was still not paying much, if anything, but Poe kept at it. He wrote several of his best works during this period.

Memorable Poems

"Eldorado" was published in the *Flag*. It told of a "gallant knight" searching "in sunshine and in shadow" for El Dorado, a mythical city filled with gold. Poe's knight never found El Dorado. The poem may have been a metaphor for the writer's life. Poe had long searched for riches he had as a child. They always eluded him.

In 1849, he also wrote a long poem called "The Bells." Here, he used repetition of the word "bells" to get his point across. The use is symbolic of the repeating of sounds bells make in real life.

> *Keeping time, time, time,*
> *In a sort of Runic rhyme,*
> *To the throbbing of the bells—*
> *Of the bells, bells, bells—*
> *To the sobbing of the bells;*
> *Keeping time, time, time,*
> *As he knells, knells, knells,*
> *In a happy Runic rhyme,*
> *To the rolling of the bells—*
> *Of the bells, bells, bells—*
> *To the tolling of the bells,*
> *Of the bells, bells, bells, bells,*
> *Bells, bells, bells—*
> *To the moaning and the groaning of the bells.*[2]

One of the last poems Poe wrote was to his aunt and mother-in-law, Muddy Clemm. It was called "Sonnet—To My Mother." In it, Poe talks about how their relationship was far more important to him than the one with the biological mother he never really knew. It returned to the every-other-line rhyming pattern Poe commonly used:

> Because I feel that, in the Heavens above,
> The angels, whispering to one another,
> Can find, among their burning terms of love,
> None so devotional as that of "Mother,"
> Therefore by that dear name I long have called you—
> You who are more than mother unto me,
> And fill my heart of hearts, where Death installed you,
> In setting my Virginia's spirit free.
> My mother—my own mother, who died early,
> Was but the mother of myself; but you
> Are mother to the one I loved so dearly,
> And thus are dearer than the mother I knew.
> By that infinity with which my wife
> Was dearer to my soul than its soul-life. [3]

Pursuing His Own Magazine

Through all he had experienced, Poe never gave up hope of publishing a magazine he created. One man appeared particularly interested in helping him. In April 1849, Poe's longtime dream nearly came true. A wealthy young newspaper owner in Illinois, Edward H. N. Patterson, wrote Poe asking him how much it would cost to start the magazine of his dreams. Patterson obviously was a fan of Poe's work and praised Poe, saying, ". . . even a cheap Magazine under *your* editorial control, could be made to pay well, and at the same time exert a beneficial influence upon American Literature."[4] Poe wrote the man back with the details he was looking for.

Poe was calling his magazine *The Stylus*. He wanted it to be an expensive journal. Patterson and Poe worked out the details and it appeared to be a go. Patterson gave Poe fifty dollars so the writer could travel and gather subscribers. His magazine dream again appeared to be well under way.

Poe eventually headed to Richmond. But the happiness of starting his magazine project could not stop him from feeling

> **"It is no use to reason with me *now*; I must die."**

ill. During this time, he wrote Muddy Clemm, telling her how sick he was. He wrote, "I have been *so* ill—have had the cholera, or spasms quite as bad, and can now hardly hold the pen. . . . It is no use to reason with me *now*; I must die."[5]

Traveling south from New York to Richmond, Poe stopped in Philadelphia. His actions there were odd and unpredictable. He begged one man for help because he said two men on a train were planning to kill him.[6] Poe later told the man the planned murder was not real, that it was all from his imagination. Poe also told people he had spent a short amount of time in prison. Records from the jail do not show his name, but he did write Clemm to tell her he had been in prison. Poe was

THE

STYLUS

A

Monthly Journal of Literature Prober

The Fine Arts And The Drama.

Aureus aliquando STYLUS, ferreus, aliquando.

Paulus Jovius.

EDITED BY

EDGAR A. POE

Poe designed what he wanted the cover of The Stylus *to look like.*

known to exaggerate but usually did not lie to Clemm. He told her it was because the police thought he was drunk. Poe said he was not drunk, but was acting oddly enough to make the police think he was because of "Virginia."[7] It was clear he still was grieving over his dead wife. He also wrote Clemm and told her how sick he was.

Poe eventually made it to Richmond, where he continued trying to establish his magazine. He was well received when he returned, and newspapers wrote about his arrival. One wrote, ". . . we know of no other writer in the United States who has half the chance to be remembered in literary history."[8] The papers had many reasons to speak well of the writer. The lectures he gave there were to packed houses, which often gave him standing ovations when he finished. If he was sick and constantly drinking, as many believe he was, he was able to fool hundreds of people. He even joined a group called The Sons of Temperance to help him stop drinking. In the smaller town where he had grown up, Poe was still a hero.

A Face From the Past

As such, most were glad to see him back in Richmond. Those happy people included Elmira Royster, his longtime love interest. Royster was thirty-nine and a widow with two children. Her husband had left her a large amount of money when he died. One day, Poe arrived unannounced at her door and the two rekindled their relationship. They still cared for each other.

For the third time, Poe asked her to marry him. In September 1849, she agreed to do so.[9]

At the end of September, Poe left Richmond for New York to get Clemm. He wanted her to come to the wedding and move in with the new bride and groom. Poe never made it there. He also planned to stop in Philadelphia on the way. He most likely never made it there, either.

A Strange End

Poe was back in Baltimore on October 3, where he was found in bad shape outside a tavern that was being used as a polling place for voters. The man who found him asked Poe if he knew anyone in the city. Poe gave the name of Dr. J. E. Snodgrass, and the man sent the doctor a note. The doctor arrived to find Poe's clothes had been taken. Instead of his customary black wool suit, Poe was wearing ragged garments and a cheap hat and carrying a walking stick. Although Poe was poor, he rarely wore grubby clothes. Many believe the ones he was wearing were not his own. His clothes were not the only things out of the ordinary. The doctor wrote, ". . . his whole physique [was] repulsive."[10]

Poe's uncle, Henry Herring, soon joined Dr. Snodgrass at the tavern. Herring suggested Poe be taken to a hospital. The two carried him into a horse-drawn carriage. When Poe arrived at the hospital, he was sweating and trembling. He had no idea where he was or who had brought him there. It was later discovered he had arrived in Baltimore by steamboat.

Still, no one knows exactly what happened to him in Baltimore, and Poe never was able to explain it.

Poe's four days in the hospital were spent in a state of confusion. Poe's doctor later wrote, ". . . I found him in a violent delirium, resisting the efforts of two nurses to keep him in bed."[11] On Poe's last night in the hospital, he kept repeating the name "Reynolds." No one knew who Reynolds was. On October 7, Poe

This is likely the door to the tavern where Poe was found under mysterious circumstances.

said, "Lord help my poor soul!"[12] Then, in the city where he had written many important works, including "MS. Found in a Bottle," which had won him fifty dollars and jump-started his career fifteen years earlier, Poe closed his eyes and died. He was forty years old.

Many believe Poe died from alcohol poisoning. Others say he died from an opium overdose. Some say he had a heart attack or brain disease. Rabies has even been mentioned. Others think Poe may have been badly beaten and died from the injuries. It was election day when Poe was found. Voting in Baltimore, and other cities, in those times often was violent and filled with criminal activities. Gangs would even capture people, change their clothes and make them go vote over and over again. The Poe Society of Baltimore's Web site talks in detail about this. It says, "To ensure compliance, their victims were plied with liquor and beaten. Poe's weak heart would never have withstood such abuse."[13] There are dozens of theories as to why Poe died, though the cause probably never will be proven.

An Unmarked Grave

Poe's funeral took place the day after his death at a cemetery in Baltimore. He was buried in the same lot as his grandfather. Few people showed up for the service. Dr. Snodgrass, the man who had been called to help Poe at the polling place, was there. He said the funeral was quick, and Poe was buried in a cheap coffin. The doctor said it did not seem right to see a man who had once been so popular be buried in such a disrespectful manner. Poe's grave was left unmarked.

The two most important people in Poe's life were not there. In fact, they did not even know he had died until after his burial. His fiancée, Elmira Royster, knew something was wrong because Poe had promised to send her a letter within a week and had not. In an October 9 newspaper article, the day after Poe was buried and two days after he had died, she found out why. The paper read, "We regret to learn that Edgar A. Poe, Esq., the distinguished American poet, scholar and critic, died in this city yesterday morning, after an illness of four or five days."[14] Royster was crushed.

She wrote, "My heart is overwhelmed—yes, ready to burst! Oh, my dear Edgar, shall I never behold your dear face & hear your sweet voice . . ."[15]

Royster wrote those words to Poe's aunt in New York. The two women never met, but were to have lived together had Poe survived and married Royster. Like

> **"We regret to learn that Edgar A. Poe, Esq., the distinguished American poet, scholar and critic, died in this city yesterday morning."**
>
> —From an October 9, 1849, newspaper report.

Royster, Muddy Clemm read about her beloved Eddy's death in a newspaper. She had seen many rumors written about Poe and did not believe what she read because of them. So she wrote Edgar's cousin, Neilson Poe, a letter asking if it was true. It read, "If it is true God have mercy on me, for he was the last I had to cling to and love . . ."[16]

Poe was used to losing the women he loved. This time, two women he loved, and the rest of the world that treasured his writing, lost him.

Remembered Evermore

A mysterious man walks across the Westminster Hall and Burying Ground cemetery in Baltimore every January 19. Dressed in black and carrying a walking stick similar to the one Poe had when he was found incoherent in Baltimore, the visitor heads for Poe's grave. When he arrives, he kneels and toasts a drink of cognac. He places a half bottle of the cognac and three red roses on the grave. Then, the mystery man leaves.

People gather to watch the early morning spectacle but rarely try to interfere. They let the man pay his tribute while observing from a distance. The man has visited the grave on the same day every year since 1949, the one hundredth anniversary of Poe's death.

A Fitting Burial

The grave the man visits is not the meager one Poe was hastily buried in the day after his death. Two decades after Poe died, his fans began raising funds to pay for a more respectable monument. In 1875, Poe's remains were removed from their original site and reburied in a corner of the same cemetery. The new marble monument there is nearly seven feet tall and surrounded by a brick walkway. Oddly, Poe's birthday on the monument is wrong. It says he was born January 20 when he was really born January 19.

Muddy Clemm, who died in 1871, is buried next to Poe. So is his wife, Virginia Poe. She was originally buried in New York, but her remains eventually were moved next to her husband's. The three people who had gone through so much together are now linked forever. Tours of the graveyard are conducted during certain times of the year, including a spooky one given each Halloween. Mystery surrounds the site. Some believe Poe's ghost haunts the cemetery. Others do not believe Poe is buried in his new grave. They say when Poe's remains were dug up and relocated across the cemetery, the diggers took the wrong ones.

This stone marks the final burial site of Edgar Allan Poe. His remains were moved to this site from another place in the same cemetery.

An Enemy After Death

The grave-visiting stranger and tourists of the Baltimore cemetery are hardly the only people who remember Poe. The writer's influence is still everywhere; the man and his words have become legendary. But, almost 160 years after his death, there are still many misconceptions about Poe. Most come from one of the first stories written about him after he died. The author was Rufus W. Griswold, and the story was known as the "Ludwig" obituary because that is the name it was published under. Griswold was an editor from New York who knew Poe. Poe once had reviewed Griswold's books, and Griswold did not like what Poe had written. Griswold had also edited some of Poe's projects. The two men did not get along. That is why many historians find it confusing that Poe reportedly told Muddy Clemm to give Griswold control of his writings after he died.

As could be predicted, this was not a good situation. Griswold wrote many untrue or rude things about Poe. He first wrote, "This announcement [of Poe's death] will startle many, but few will be grieved by it."[1] Griswold also compiled and edited a three-volume book called *The Works of the Late Edgar Allan Poe*. The book was published in 1850. In it, Griswold continued bashing the dead man. He lied, made up facts, and embellished points to make Poe sound worse than he was. Many felt Griswold was trying to pay Poe back because of jealousy. It was easy to do because Poe, of course, was not around to defend himself. He surely would have if he had been alive.

After Griswold's words were printed, those who knew Poe came to the dead man's defense. Griswold's story was repeated and spread across the world. Future biographers, including John Henry Ingram in 1874, tried to set the record straight. Most who have read all the facts now believe Poe was a decent, hard-working man with a talent far ahead of his time. But many also still believe Poe was nothing but a lying, greedy drunkard and drug addict, often because of Griswold's malicious words. Poe did drink and often stretched the truth. But many who knew him have said those negative traits were only a small part of what he was all about. Still, Poe's reputation suffered for many years, and often still does, because of Griswold.

Poe's cousin, Dr. Harry L. Poe, said:

> *Poe's biographer and editor turned out to be his enemy. He lied about Poe in the official biography that was printed with the works of Poe throughout the nineteenth century. As a result, few people know what Poe was like. Poe scholars have tried to correct the popular image, but it is difficult to correct a myth once it has become part of popular culture.*[2]

In spite of Griswold's hurtful words, people across the world continue to read Poe's writings and study his life. Years after they were written and the author was dead, Poe's short stories, poems, and essays are still highly regarded.

Because of the language and references Poe used, his work is difficult to understand for many. Many words Poe used are not common today and were not common when he wrote them. He even created some of his own words.

Poe's work is open to different interpretations. Because the subjects he wrote about were often complex and mysterious, some believe there must be hidden meanings in his stories. His writings have been examined several times to find what they are "truly" about.

Poe's Words

Not only was Poe a master at using English words, but he also was good at creating them. Words Poe either created or made popular include:

bewinged—Having wings.

bullety—Physical description of something that is shaped like a bullet.

compassless—Not having a compass.

hackneyism—To make common or stale by frequent use.

multicolor—Having many colors.

quotability—Qualified to be quoted.[3]

Poe is considered the creator of the detective story and of science fiction. Many generations of writers in those genres cite Poe as an inspiration. Sherlock Holmes, a character in a series of detective books by Sir Arthur Conan Doyle, is patterned after Poe's sleuth, C. Auguste Dupin.

When Poe was alive, it was his poetry people knew best. After all, "The Raven" was what made him wildly popular. However, most people today know Poe for his horror stories. They are attracted to their disturbing, haunting, and shadowy nature.

Movie director Alfred Hitchcock, known for his classic suspense films such as *Vertigo*, *The Birds*, and *Psycho*, has cited Poe as the reason he started doing what he did. Hitchcock himself has become an influence to future generations. Thus Poe has influenced those people, too.

Each year, The Mystery Writers of America gives out several awards. They are called the "Edgars." Winners receive a small statue of Poe wearing a blue jacket and a black tie.

The United States is not the only country where Poe remains influential. His works have been translated into more than a dozen languages. He is held in particularly high regard in France, the setting for "The Murders in the Rue Morgue." A lot of that was due to a poet named Charles Baudelaire who translated Poe's work into French for his countrymen to read and enjoy. Baudelaire also patterned a lot of his own work after Poe's.

Poe's literary life has come full circle. Many of his life experiences inspired his writing. Now, other writers have used Poe in their stories. Poe has become a fictional character, like the ones he wrote about. The first movie he "appeared" in as a character was a silent film in 1909.[4] Actor Vincent Price starred in a series of successful films from the 1960s based on Poe's works. They include "The Fall of the House of Usher," "The Pit and the Pendulum," "Tales of Terror," "The Raven," and "The City Under the Sea."[5]

Poe also is influential outside the field of writing and film. Other forms of popular culture are filled with references to Poe. The classic Beatles' album *Sgt. Pepper's Lonely Hearts Club Band* featured a photo of Poe on the cover. Many songs have been titled after Poe's

Vincent Price starred in many movies based on Edgar Allan Poe's works. This photo is from the 1960 movie House of Usher, *which was based on the story "The Fall of the House of Usher."*

works, such as "William Wilson," "The Murders in the Rue Morgue," and "The Fall of the House of Usher." Modern-day movies, such as *The Crow, Young Guns*, and *The Lost Boys* have borrowed from Poe's works. TV shows such as *The Simpsons, CSI*, and *The Gilmore Girls* have, too. Popular rock bands, such as Good Charlotte and Green Day, reference his name or his words in their lyrics.[6] Sylvester Stallone, famous for his "Rocky" movies featuring an overachieving boxer, is writing a major film about Poe's life. It is scheduled to be released in theaters in 2009.

Poe—the man and his writing—is taught as a subject in many schools. About his cousin's influence, Dr. Harry L. Poe said:

> *Poe may have been dead for a long time, but English teachers around the country tell us that their classes come alive when they get to the section on Poe. Poe continues to communicate with young people. Because Poe has been misunderstood and criticized, many young people identify with him and see him as their own. He deals with themes of lost love, death, internalized emotions, rejection, human failure and mistreatment of others in such a way that young people connect with him.*[7]

There are Edgar Allan Poe T-shirts, comic books, postcards, dolls, and figurines. His room at the University of Virginia is not the only site for people to visit. Houses where Poe lived in Philadelphia and Baltimore are preserved for historic purposes. His house in Philadelphia, for example, is now a National Historic

Site operated by the United States National Park Service. There, you can take tours and learn more about the man. On his birthday and near Halloween, there are candlelight tours and his poems often are acted out to music. A large raven on a post greets visitors.

The Poe Museum in Richmond, Virginia, claims to have the world's best collection of Poe's books, letters, and personal items. Many weddings are held in the museum's garden. Each summer, the museum sponsors the Edgar Allan Poe Young Writers' Conference for students entering tenth, eleventh, and twelfth grade. Attendees spend a week writing, hearing lectures, and learning about Poe. Dr. Harry L. Poe has been the museum's president since 2002. Dr. Poe is a writer himself and also leads the conference, which draws kids from across the United States.

The tiny farmhouse where Edgar Allan and Virginia Poe and Muddy Clemm lived is also a historical house. It is called the Edgar Allan Poe Cottage. It is located in The Bronx section of New York City. It was the last place Poe lived.

This brick building, where Poe lived from 1833 to 1835, is now a museum in Baltimore called the Edgar Allan Poe House. It has been designated a National Historic Landmark.

Edgar Allan Poe's legacy will live on in his memorable short stories and poems.

The house was saved from demolition and restored in the early 1900s. It looks nearly the same inside and out as it did when the famous family lived there. It rests in the middle of Poe Park.

The city of Baltimore is filled with Poe references. The Baltimore Ravens football team, for example, is named after his most famous poem. The team's mascots are three people dressed as the famous fictional bird. Their names are Edgar, Allan, and Poe. The brick house where Poe lived was supposed to be demolished in the 1930s, but has since been renovated and is now the Edgar Allan Poe House. Tours are given year-round, and the house is close enough to his grave that it is easy to visit both.

Today, Poe is known for many different reasons. He was a misunderstood man who made little money when he was alive. Poe's last years, much like his first, were filled with desperation and poverty. In his final year of life, he made $275. In forty years, Poe made a total of $6,200 from writing.[8] That would equal roughly $100,000 today.

He may not have made a lot of money, but Poe accomplished one thing most people never will. Some 160 years after his death, he is still world famous. When Poe was alive, his writings helped him understand his mixed-up world and gave him many imaginary places to escape to. As long as people continue to appreciate the misunderstood and mysterious man and his literary works of genius, they, too, will continue to escape into his writings for many years to come. Possibly, for evermore.

"THE RAVEN" by Edgar Allan Poe

Once upon a midnight dreary, while I pondered, weak and weary,
Over many a quaint and curious volume of forgotten lore—
While I nodded, nearly napping, suddenly there came a tapping,
As of some one gently rapping—rapping at my chamber door.
"'Tis some visitor," I muttered, "tapping at my chamber door—
Only this and nothing more."

Ah, distinctly I remember, it was in the bleak December,
And each separate dying ember wrought its ghost upon the floor.
Eagerly I wished the morrow; —vainly I had sought to borrow
From my books surcease of sorrow—sorrow for the lost Lenore—
For the rare and radiant maiden whom the angels name Lenore—
Nameless here for evermore.

And the silken sad uncertain rustling of each purple curtain
Thrilled me—filled me with fantastic terrors never felt before;
So that now, to still the beating of my heart, I stood repeating
"'Tis some visitor entreating entrance at my chamber door—
Some late visitor entreating entrance at my chamber door;—
This it is and nothing more."

Presently my soul grew stronger; hesitating then no longer,
"Sir," said I, "or Madam, truly your forgiveness I implore;
But the fact is I was napping, and so gently you came rapping,
And so faintly you came tapping—tapping at my chamber door,
That I scarce was sure I heard you"—here I opened wide the door:—
Darkness there and nothing more.

Deep into that darkness peering, long I stood there wondering, fearing,
Doubting, dreaming dreams no mortal ever dared to dream before;
But the silence was unbroken, and the darkness gave no token,
And the only word there spoken was the whispered word, "Lenore!"
This I whispered, and an echo murmured back the word, "Lenore!"
Merely this and nothing more.

Back into the chamber turning, all my soul within me burning,
Soon I heard again a tapping, somewhat louder than before.
"Surely," said I, "surely that is something at my window lattice;
Let me see, then, what thereat is, and this mystery explore—
Let my heart be still a moment, and this mystery explore;—
'Tis the wind and nothing more."

Open here I flung the shutter, when, with many a flirt and flutter,
In there stepped a stately Raven of the saintly days of yore;
Not the least obeisance made he: not an instant stopped
    or stayed he;
But, with mien of lord or lady, perched above my
    chamber door—
Perched upon a bust of Pallas just above my
    chamber door—
Perched, and sat, and nothing more.

Then this ebony bird beguiling my sad fancy into smiling,
By the grave and stern decorum of the countenance it wore,
"Though thy crest be shorn and shaven, thou,"
    I said, "art sure no craven,

Ghastly grim and ancient Raven wandering from the Nightly shore—
Tell me what thy lordly name is on the Night's Plutonian shore!"
Quoth the Raven, "Nevermore."

Much I marvelled this ungainly fowl
to hear discourse so plainly,
Though its answer little meaning—little relevancy bore;
For we cannot help agreeing that no living human being
Ever yet was blessed with seeing bird above his chamber door—
Bird or beast upon the sculptured bust above his chamber door,
With such name as "Nevermore."

But the Raven, sitting lonely on that placid bust, spoke only
That one word, as if his soul in that one word he did outpour.
Nothing further then he uttered—not a feather then he fluttered—
Till I scarcely more than muttered, "Other friends have flown before—
On the morrow he will leave me, as my hopes have flown before."
Then the bird said, "Nevermore."

Startled at the stillness broken by reply so aptly spoken,
"Doubtless," said I, "what it utters is its only stock
    and store,
Caught from some unhappy master whom unmerciful
    Disaster
Followed fast and followed faster till his songs one
    burden bore—
Till the dirges of his Hope the melancholy burden bore
Of 'Never—nevermore.'"

But the Raven still beguiling all my sad soul into smiling,
Straight I wheeled a cushioned seat in front of bird and bust and door;
Then, upon the velvet sinking, I betook myself to linking
Fancy unto fancy, thinking what this ominous bird of yore—
What this grim, ungainly, ghastly, gaunt, and ominous bird of yore
Meant in croaking "Nevermore."

This I sat engaged in guessing, but no syllable expressing
To the fowl whose fiery eyes now burned into my bosom's core;
This and more I sat divining, with my head at ease reclining
On the cushion's velvet lining that the lamp-light gloated o'er,
But whose velvet violet lining with the lamp-light gloating o'er,
She *shall* press, ah, nevermore!

Then, methought, the air grew denser, perfumed from an unseen censer
Swung by Seraphim whose foot-falls tinkled on the tufted floor.
"Wretch," I cried, "thy God hath lent thee—by these angels he hath sent thee
Respite—respite and nepenthé from thy memories of Lenore!
Quaff, oh quaff this kind nepenthé, and forget this lost Lenore!"
Quoth the Raven, "Nevermore."

"Prophet!" said I, "thing of evil!—prophet still, if bird or devil!—
Whether Tempter sent, or whether tempest tossed thee here ashore,
Desolate yet all undaunted, on this desert land enchanted—
On this home by Horror haunted—tell me truly, I implore—
Is there—is there balm in Gilead?—tell me—tell me, I implore!"
Quoth the Raven, "Nevermore."

"Prophet!" said I, "thing of evil!—prophet still, if bird or devil!
By that Heaven that bends above us — by that God we both adore—
Tell this soul with sorrow laden if, within the distant Aidenn,
It shall clasp a sainted maiden whom the angels name Lenore —
Clasp a rare and radiant maiden whom the angels name Lenore."
Quoth the Raven, "Nevermore."

"Be that word our sign of parting, bird or fiend!" I shrieked, upstarting—
"Get thee back into the tempest and the Night's Plutonian shore!
Leave no black plume as a token of that lie thy soul hath spoken!
Leave my loneliness unbroken!—quit the bust above my door!
Take thy beak from out my heart, and take thy form from off my door!"
Quoth the Raven, "Nevermore."

And the Raven, never flitting, still is sitting, still is sitting
On the pallid bust of Pallas just above my chamber door;
And his eyes have all the seeming of a demon's that is dreaming,
And the lamp-light o'er him streaming throws his shadow on the floor;
And my soul from out that shadow that lies floating on the floor
Shall be lifted—nevermore!

Source: Edgar Allan Poe, "The Raven," *Project Gutenberg*, November 10, 2003, <http://www.gutenberg.org/files/10031/10031-h/10031-h.htm#section2c> (November 16, 2006).

AMERICANS—*The Spirit of a Nation*

CHRONOLOGY

1809—Born January 19, in Boston to David Poe Jr. and Elizabeth Arnold Poe.

1810—Father deserts family; Edgar moves with family to Richmond, Virginia; sister, Rosalie, born.

1811—Mother dies of tuberculosis; taken in by John and Fanny Allan; name changes from Edgar Poe to Edgar Allan Poe.

1815–1820—Travels by boat to Great Britain with the Allans; attends boarding schools of the Misses Dubourg and the Reverend John Bransby; returns with Allans to Richmond.

1821—Attends school of Joseph H. Clarke.

1823—Attends school of William Burke; meets Jane Stanard, mother of a fellow student.

1824—Jane Stanard dies.

1825—Gets secretly engaged to Elmira Royster.

1826—Enters the University of Virginia; Elmira Royster's father breaks off couple's engagement; incurs gambling debts; feuds with another student; leaves University of Virginia to return to Richmond.

1827—Feuds with John Allan; moves to Boston; publishes *Tamerlane and Other Poems*; enlists in U.S. Army.

1829—Promoted to sergeant major; Fanny Allan dies; discharged from Army in April; publishes *Al Aaraaf, Tamerlane and Minor Poems*.

1830—Enters West Point.

1831—Dismissed from West Point; publishes *Poems*; older brother, Henry Poe, dies; moves to Baltimore to live with family members.

1832—Five short stories published in *Philadelphia Saturday Courier*.

1833—Short story, "MS. Found in a Bottle," wins fifty dollars in a contest.

1834—John Allan dies; publishes several stories in *Southern Literary Messenger*.

1835—Named owner's assistant at *Southern Literary Messenger*, earning ten dollars a week; moves back to Richmond; professes love for thirteen-year-old cousin, Virginia Clemm; quits job at *Southern Literary Messenger* to return to Baltimore to ask for Virginia's hand in marriage; returns to work at *Southern Literary Messenger*.

1836—Weds Virginia; *Southern Literary Messenger* flourishes under Poe's leadership.

1837—Quits job at *Southern Literary Messenger*; moves to New York.

1838—Moves to Philadelphia; publishes *The Narrative of Arthur Gordon Pym*.

1839—Goes to work for *Burton's Gentleman's Magazine*, publishing "The Fall of the House of Usher" and "William Wilson" there; publishes *Tales of the Grotesque and Arabesque*.

1840—Fired from *Burton's* after announcing plans to start his own publication, *Penn Magazine*.

1841—Publishes several of own writings in *Graham's Magazine*, including "The Murders in the Rue Morgue"; becomes editor of *Graham's*.

1842—Virginia Poe grows ill; quits working at *Graham's*.

1843—Short story "The Gold-Bug" wins one hundred dollars in contest.

1844—Returns to New York; publishes "The Balloon-Hoax"; moves with family to farm outside New York City; goes to work for New York *Evening Mirror* newspaper; feuds with Henry Wadsworth Longfellow.

1845—*Evening Mirror* publishes "The Raven"; leaves *Evening Mirror* to work for the *Broadway Journal*; begins getting paid to make public speeches; publishes *Tales*; publishes *The Raven and Other Poems*; purchases the *Broadway Journal*.

1846—The *Broadway Journal* publishes its last issue; begins to drink heavily; publishes "The Literati of New York City."

1847—Wife, Virginia, dies of tuberculosis at age twenty-four; wins more than $225 in a lawsuit; grows ill and becomes reclusive.

1848—Renews attempt to start his own magazine, calling it *The Stylus*; publishes *Eureka*; gets engaged to Sarah Helen Whitman; Whitman breaks off engagement; stays with Nancy Richmond and husband.

1849—Publishes several poems, including "Eldorado," and "Sonnet—To My Mother"; travels from New York to Richmond; gets engaged to childhood sweetheart, Elmira Royster; stops in Baltimore on return to New York; begins drinking heavily; discovered in poor shape outside a tavern and brought to a hospital; dies October 7.

CHAPTER NOTES

CHAPTER 1
A Grand Prize

1. The Edgar Allan Poe Society of Baltimore, August 1, 1998, <http://www.eapoe.org/balt/poebalt.htm> (October 10, 2006).
2. Dwight Thomas and David K. Jackson, *The Poe Log: A Documentary Life of Edgar Allan Poe 1809–1849* (New York: G.K. Hall & Co., 1987), p. 129.
3. Ibid.
4. Ibid.
5. Ibid.
6. Arthur Hobson Quinn, *Edgar Allan Poe: A Critical Biography* (Baltimore: The Johns Hopkins University Press, 1998), p. 204.

CHAPTER 2
Changing Names

1. Jeffrey Meyers, *Edgar Allan Poe: His Life & Legacy* (New York: Charles Scribner's Sons, 1992), p. 3.
2. Ibid.
3. Arthur Hobson Quinn, *Edgar Allan Poe: A Critical Biography* (Baltimore: The Johns Hopkins University Press, 1998), p. 704.
4. Meyers, p. 3.
5. Quinn, p. 13.
6. "Tuberculosis Symptoms," WebMD, May 25, 2005, <http://www.webmd.com/hw/infection/hw207352.asp> (August 30, 2007).

7. Dwight Thomas and David K. Jackson, *The Poe Log: A Documentary Life of Edgar Allan Poe 1809–1849* (New York: G.K. Hall & Co., 1987), pp. 3–4.

CHAPTER 3
Early Talent

1. Arthur Hobson Quinn, *Edgar Allan Poe: A Critical Biography* (Baltimore: The Johns Hopkins University Press, 1998), p. 60.
2. Gorton Carruth, *The Encyclopedia of American Facts and Dates, Tenth Edition* (New York: HarperCollins, 1997), p. 9.
3. Ibid.
4. Dwight Thomas and David K. Jackson, *The Poe Log: A Documentary Life of Edgar Allan Poe 1809–1849* (New York: G.K. Hall & Co., 1987), p. 32.
5. Jeffrey Meyers, *Edgar A. Poe: His Life & Legacy* (New York: Charles Scribner's Sons, 1992), p. 13.
6. Thomas and Jackson, p. 39.
7. Meyers, p. 13.
8. Ibid., p. 14–15.
9. Ibid.
10. Edgar Allan Poe, "To Helen," From "Poems of Youth," *Project Gutenberg*, November 10, 2003, <http://www.gutenberg.org/files/10031/10031-h/10031-h.htm#section2k> (August 27, 2007).
11. Meyers, p. 18.
12. Edgar Allan Poe, "Song," *Project Gutenberg*, November 10, 2003, <http://www.gutenberg.org/files/10031/10031-h/10031-h.htm#section5k> (August 27, 2007).
13. Meyers, p. 18.

CHAPTER 4
School's Out

1. "September 21, 1826, from Edgar Allan Poe to John Allan," *The University of Virginia Library*, n.d., <http://

etext.lib.virginia.edu/etcbin/toccer-new2?id=PoeVal2.sg
m&images=images/modeng&data=/texts/english/mode
ng/parsed&tag=public&part=1&division=div1>
(December 6, 2006).

2. Ibid.

3. "Letter from Edgar Allan Poe to Mr. John Allan,
January 3, 1831," *The University of Virginia Library*, n.d.,
<http://etext.lib.virginia.edu/etcbin/toccer-new2?id=Poe
Va24.sgm&images=images/modeng&data=/texts/englis
h/modeng/parsed&tag=public&part=1&division=
div1> (December 6, 2006).

4. Personal interview with Ross Baird, January 16, 2007.

5. Ibid.

6. Jeffrey Meyers, *Edgar Allan Poe: His Life & Legacy* (New
York: Charles Scribner's Sons, Macmillan Publishing
Company, 1992), p. 20.

7. Personal interview with Ross Baird, January 16, 2007.

8. Meyers, p. 20.

9. Personal interview with Ross Baird, January 16, 2007.

10. Ibid.

11. Dwight Thomas and David K. Jackson, *The Poe Log: A
Documentary Life of Edgar Allan Poe 1809-1849* (New York:
G.K. Hall & Co., 1987), p. 78.

12. "Letter from Edgar Allan Poe Richmond to John Allan,
dated March 20, 1827," *The University of Virginia Library*,
n.d., <http://etext.lib.virginia.edu/etcbin/toccer-new2?id
=PoeVal04.sgm&images=images/modeng&data=/texts/
english/modeng/parsed&tag=public&part=1&division
=div1> (December 7, 2006).

13. Edgar Allan Poe, "Tamerlane," *Project Gutenberg*,
November 10, 2003, <http://www.gutenberg.org/files/10
031/10031-h/10031-h.htm#section5d> (December 6,
2006).

14. Arthur Hobson Quinn, *Edgar Allan Poe: A Critical
Biography* (Baltimore: The Johns Hopkins University
Press, 1998), p. 119.

15. Edgar Allan Poe, "The Gold-Bug," *Project Gutenberg*, June 24, 2005, <http://www.gutenberg.org/dirs/etext00/poe1v 10.txt> (November 23, 2006).

16. "Letter from Edgar Allan Poe to John Allan, 1829 February 4," *The University of Virginia Library*, n.d., <http://etext.lib.virginia.edu/etcbin/toccer-new2?id=Poe Val8.sgm&images=images/modeng&data=/texts/english /modeng/parsed&tag=public&part=1&division=div1> (December 7, 2006).

17. Quinn, p. 142.

18. Ibid., p. 169.

19. Ibid., p. 171.

20. "Fact Sheet," *The United States Military Academy West Point*, n.d., <http://www.usma.edu/PublicAffairs/Press_ Kit_files/SelectedNoteworthyGrads.htm> (September 3, 2007).

21. "Letter from Edgar Allan Poe to Mr. John Allan, January 3, 1831" *The University of Virginia Library*, n.d., <http:// etext.lib.virginia.edu/etcbin/toccer-new2?id=PoeVa24.sg m&images=images/modeng&data=/texts/english/mode ng/parsed&tag=public&part=1&division=div1> (November 10, 2006).

22. Meyers, p. 51.

23. J.R. Hammond, *An Edgar Allan Poe Companion* (Totowa, N.J.: Barnes & Noble Books, 1981), p. 14.

CHAPTER 5
Writing to Live

1. Arthur Hobson Quinn, *Edgar Allan Poe: A Critical Biography* (Baltimore: The Johns Hopkins University Press, 1998), p. 206.

2. Ibid., p. 219.

3. Ibid., pp. 223–224.

4. Ibid., p. 224

5. Ibid., pp. 228–229.

6. Dwight Thomas and David K. Jackson, *The Poe Log: A Documentary Life of Edgar Allan Poe 1809–1849* (New York: G.K. Hall & Co., 1987), p. 206.
7. Quinn, p. 260.
8. Personal interview with Dr. Harry L. Poe, January 18, 2007.
9. Ibid.
10. Ibid.
11. Ibid.
12. Edgar Allan Poe, "The Fall of the House of Usher," *Project Gutenberg*, February 27, 2003, <http://www.gutenberg.org/dirs/etext97/usher10h.htm> (September 3, 2003).
13. Edgar Allan Poe, "William Wilson," *Project Gutenberg*, December 9, 2005, <http://www.gutenberg.org/dirs/etext00/poe2v10.txt> (September 1, 2007).

CHAPTER 6
Quoth the Raven

1. Bettina L. Knapp, *Edgar Allan Poe* (New York: Ungar, 1984), p. 30.
2. Edgar Allan Poe, "The Murders in the Rue Morgue," *Project Gutenberg*, June 23, 2005, <http://www.gutenberg.org/dirs/etext00/poe1v10.txt> (August 25, 2007).
3. Arthur Hobson Quinn, *Edgar Allan Poe: A Critical Biography* (Baltimore: The Johns Hopkins University Press, 1998), p. 341.
4. Ibid., pp. 474–475.
5. Knapp, p. 32.
6. Jeffrey Meyers, *Edgar Allan Poe: His Life & Legacy* (New York: Charles Scribner's Sons, 1992), p. 89.
7. Edgar Allan Poe, "The Pit and the Pendulum," *Project Gutenberg*, December 9, 2005, <http://www.gutenberg.org/dirs/etext00/poe2v10.txt> (August 30, 2007).
8. Edgar Allan Poe, "The Tell-Tale Heart," *Project Gutenberg*, December 9, 2005, <http://www.gutenberg.org/dirs/etext00/poe2v10.txt> (August 31, 2007).

9. Dwight Thomas and David K. Jackson, *The Poe Log: A Documentary Life of Edgar Allan Poe 1809–1849* (New York: G.K. Hall & Co., 1987), p. 461.
10. Meyers, p. 171.
11. Quinn, p. 410.
12. Thomas and Jackson, p. 497.
13. Meyers, p. 183.
14. J.R. Hammond, *An Edgar Allan Poe Companion* (Totowa, N.J.: Barnes & Noble Books, 1981), p. 20.
15. Ibid.

CHAPTER 7
Rough Times

1. Jeffrey Meyers, *Edgar Allan Poe: His Life & Legacy* (New York: Charles Scribner's Sons, 1992), p. 188.
2. Dwight Thomas and David K. Jackson, *The Poe Log: A Documentary Life of Edgar Allan Poe 1809–1849* (New York: G.K. Hall & Co., 1987), p. 639.
3. Meyers, p. 192.
4. Edgar Allan Poe, "The Literati," (Part V), *The Edgar Allan Poe Society of Baltimore*, December 13, 2000, <http://www.eapoe.org/WorkS/misc/litratd6.htm#E:Hoffman,%20C> (December 25, 2006).
5. Arthur Hobson Quinn, *Edgar Allan Poe: A Critical Biography* (Baltimore: The Johns Hopkins University Press, 1998), p. 510.
6. Ibid., p. 525.
7. Ibid.
8. Ibid.
9. Meyers, p. 205.
10. Edgar Allan Poe, "Ulalume," *Project Gutenberg*, November 10, 2003, <http://www.gutenberg.org/files/10031/10031-h/10031-h.htm#section2e> (October 16, 2006).
11. Edgar Allan Poe, "To Helen," *Project Gutenberg*, November 10, 2003, <http://www.gutenberg.org/files/10031/10031-h/10031-h.htm#section2f> (October 16, 2006).
12. Quinn, p. 592.

13. Edgar Allan Poe, "For Annie," *Project Gutenberg*, November 10, 2003, <http://www.gutenberg.org/files/10 031/10031-h/10031-h.htm#section2k> (October 27, 2006).

CHAPTER 8
Final Days

1. Jeffrey Meyers, *Edgar Allan Poe: His Life & Legacy* (New York: Charles Scribner's Sons, 1992), p. 237.
2. Edgar Allan Poe, "The Bells," *Project Gutenberg*, November 10, 2003, <http://www.gutenberg.org/files/10 031/10031-h/10031-h.htm#section2d> (January 1, 2007).
3. Edgar Allan Poe, "To My Mother," *Project Gutenberg*, November 10, 2003, <http://www.gutenberg.org/files/10 031/10031-h/10031-h.htm#section2j> (January 2, 2007).
4. Dwight Thomas and David K. Jackson, *The Poe Log: A Documentary Life of Edgar Allan Poe 1809–1849* (New York: G.K. Hall & Co., 1987), p. 803.
5. Ibid., p. 814.
6. Arthur Hobson Quinn, *Edgar Allan Poe: A Critical Biography* (Baltimore: The Johns Hopkins University Press, 1998), p. 616.
7. Ibid., p. 618.
8. John Evangelist Walsh, *Midnight Dreary: The Mysterious Death of Edgar Allan Poe* (New Brunswick, N.J.: Rutgers University Press, 1998), p. 19.
9. Thomas and Jackson, pp. 838–839.
10. Meyers, p. 253.
11. Thomas and Jackson, p. 846.
12. Meyers, p. 255.
13. *The Edgar Allan Poe Society of Baltimore*, August 1, 1998, <http://www.eapoe.org/geninfo/poedeath.htm> (October 4, 2007).
14. Walsh, p. 34.
15. Ibid., p. 35.

16. Thomas and Jackson, p. 850.

CHAPTER 9
Remembered Evermore

1. Arthur Hobson Quinn, *Edgar Allan Poe: A Critical Biography* (Baltimore: The Johns Hopkins University Press, 1998), p. 646.
2. Personal interview with Dr. Harry L. Poe, January 18, 2007.
3. Burton R. Pollin, *Poe: Creator of Words* (Baltimore: Enoch Pratt Free Library and the Edgar Allan Poe Society of Baltimore, 1974), pp. 23–35.
4. *The Edgar Allan Poe Society of Baltimore*, "Poe Film Poster No. 1," October 11, 1997, <http://www.eapoe.org/gen info/poef008a.htm> (January 12, 2007).
5. Ibid.
6. *Qrisse's Poe Pages*, "Edgar Allan Poe's Footprints," February 13, 2007, <http://www.poedecoder.com/Qrisse/ footprints.php> (August 30, 2007).
7. Personal interview with Dr. Harry L. Poe, January 18, 2007.
8. Jeffrey Meyers, *Edgar Allan Poe: His Life & Legacy* (New York: Charles Scribner's Sons, 1992), p. 186.

GLOSSARY

anthology—A collection of writings, such as poems, plays, or short stories.

boarding school—A school where students eat and live.

critic—A person who expresses opinions of artistic works such as musical performances, plays, stories, and more.

depression—An often clinical state of sadness and gloom.

editor—A person who examines writings for publications and often makes managerial decisions on such content.

engaged—Promised to be married.

enlist—To enroll, usually voluntarily, for military service.

fiction—Stories that are untrue and have been invented.

gothic—A style of fiction that emphasizes the mysterious and grotesque.

harbor—A part of a body of water along a shore deep enough for ships to anchor in.

impoverished—Poor.

inheritance—Something, often money, passed down from one relative to another.

metaphor—Something used to represent something else.

narrator—A person telling a story.

orphan—A child who is without parents.

plot—The main idea of a play, short story, novel, or other piece of literature.

prospectus—A document describing the major features of a plan.

publish—To bring a printed material to the general public, often for distribution or sale.

review—A critique of a piece of artistic work, such as a play, short story, or novel.

tradesman—A worker who is skilled in a particular craft.

tuberculosis—An often deadly infectious disease commonly affecting the lungs.

widow—A woman whose husband has died and who has not remarried.

FURTHER READING

Collections of Works by Poe

Delbanco, Andrew, ed. *Edgar Allan Poe.* New York: Sterling Pub. Co., 2006.

Poe, Edgar Allan. *The Raven and Other Poems and Stories.* Franklin Watts, 2007.

Books About Poe

Bloom, Harold, ed. *Edgar Allan Poe.* New York: Chelsea House Publishers, 2006.

Frisch, Aaron. *Edgar Allan Poe.* Mankato, Minn.: Creative Education, 2006.

Streissguth, Tom. *Edgar Allan Poe.* Minneapolis: Lerner Publications Co., 2007.

Whiting, Jim. *Edgar Allan Poe.* Hockessin, Del.: Mitchell Lane Publishers, 2006.

INTERNET ADDRESSES

Edgar Allan Poe Museum
   <http://www.poemuseum.org>

Edgar Allan Poe Society of Baltimore
   <http://www.eapoe.org>

Project Gutenberg: Poe, Edgar Allan, 1809–1849
   <http://www.gutenberg.org/browse/authors
   /p#a481>

INDEX